PAUL A. JOHNSGARD

Sandhill and Whooping Cranes
Ancient Voices over America's Wetlands

UNIVERSITY OF NEBRASKA PRESS | LINCOLN & LONDON

Library of Congress Cataloging-in-
Publication Data
Johnsgard, Paul A.
Sandhill and whooping cranes:
ancient voices over America's wetlands
/ Paul A. Johnsgard.
p.   cm.
Includes bibliographical references
and index.
ISBN 978-0-8032-3496-3
(pbk.: alk. paper)
1. Sandhill crane. 2. Whooping crane.
I. Title.
QL696.G84J626   2011
598.3'2—dc22
2010025807

Set in ITC New Baskerville
by Bob Reitz.

To those for whom crane voices
speak a language that resonates
more strongly and more personally
than any human voice, and whose
messages change their lives

Contents

Illustrations

Maps

Preface

I experienced unadulterated magic some years ago when for the first time I took my seven-year-old grand-daughter to see the sandhill cranes on the Platte River. She had been asking me to take her for several years, indeed ever since my daughter explained that the cranes I spend so much time watching each year weren't the kind of machinery cranes she already knew about. Finally, after some advice on using binoculars, I felt she was ready.

We arrived on the Platte very early one Saturday morning in late March, as night slowly was giving way to dawn. The planet Mars was high in the sky, Venus was brilliant in the eastern sky, and the moon was approaching fullness. Great horned owls sang occasional duets, and the roosting cranes talked to one another with increasing urgency. We settled into hiding places in the tall grasses a few hundred yards downstream from a crane roost.

Then, just before sunrise, the cranes rose majestically in flock after flock, along with even larger groups of Canada geese, and headed toward feeding grounds south of the river. To one who has never experienced such a scene, it is nearly impossible to convey, but standing beside railroad tracks as a speeding locomotive passes by may give some slight idea of the sound and implicit power expressed in the takeoff of ten thousand cranes.

We spent the rest of the day in the quiet pleasures

of nature, looking for the first signs of insect life in the prairie grasses, at the abandoned nests of goldfinches, song sparrows, and blackbirds that were still firmly attached to the branches of rose, plum, and dogwood bushes along roadside ditches, and listened for the songs of mourning doves and robins emanating from nearby woodlots. And we patiently waited for the sun to set, to provide the second act of the sandhill crane's Platte River drama.

xii

The daily return of the cranes to the river near sunset is not so much a sudden explosion as a gradual build-up of tension and beauty, in a manner resembling Ravel's "Bolero." As the western skies redden, the cranes fly up and down the main channel of the river, calling with gradually increasing urgency, evidently trying to decide where they might most safely spend their night. Sometimes the weak, chirping voice of a yearling crane, seemingly worried about being separated from its parents in the evening confusion, penetrates the general level of crane conversation. The decision to land is finally made by a few adventuresome souls, and the rest of the birds tumble in behind, all calling at the tops of their lungs. My granddaughter was almost at a loss for words, but finally ventured to timidly ask, "Grandpa, do the cranes only do this on Saturday nights?"

Returning each spring to the central Platte Valley to observe the migration of a half-million sandhill cranes is a mind-shattering experience that can only be had in Nebraska, and only by making a special effort to participate in it.

From the time the Platte River becomes ice-free in February, until almost the middle of April, hundreds of thousands of sandhill cranes use the valley every year, the largest assemblage by far of any cranes in the world. Along dozens of the more remote stretches of river, nightly roosts of up to 20,000 birds gather to spend the night standing in shallow waters. They select the widest stretches of river that offer nearly vegetation-free sandy islands and sandbars, which places them out of danger of land-based predators such as coyotes.

Nobody knows what originally drew the cranes to the Platte, but the unique present-day combination of a wide, sandy river, nearby wet meadows with a supply of invertebrate foods for a source of calcium and protein, and an almost unlimited amount of waste corn in nearby fields for getting abundant carbohydrates that can be converted and stored as fat provide the magic attraction now. Millions of snow geese, Ross's geese, Canada geese, and greater white-fronted geese join in on this feast, as do several million ducks, making March in Nebraska a bird-watcher's paradise. Its prospect is enough to warm the heart during the long days of winter.

This March, like unnumbered springs before it, the cranes have again returned to the Platte Valley. Their annual predictable appearance is like watching a favorite spring flower unfolding, a theme of music developing, and a promise being fulfilled. That promise is being paid annually by the experienced migrant cranes to all the generations of cranes that have stopped in the Platte Valley in eons past.

In the midst of every Nebraska winter, I am optimistically filled with the certain expectation that by mid-February the first sandhill cranes will lift off from the playa lakes and grain stubble of New Mexico and Texas and begin drifting northward along invisible migratory routes followed for unknown millennia by their ancestors. The navigational knowledge for this massive exodus is somehow efficiently handed down year after year, generation by generation, from parents to offspring. There is majesty in all of this, made even greater by our own human inability to understand it. There is no way to predict winners and losers in the cranes' serious game of survival; only an awareness that one is being privileged to witness the day-to-day struggles for survival of a species that has somehow survived in the face of centuries of human exploitation. It is an exalting thought, and one worth keeping firmly in mind until the middle of March, when the cranes and geese will be here in all their magic and beauty.

xiv

The present generation of cranes must instill among the less experienced birds a firm memory of the Platte during their spring and fall migrations, the locations of its wet meadows, its grain fields, and a collective memory of its safe roosting sites. Then the river's frigid waters lap at the feet of the cranes as they stand all night around the edges of the Platte's sandbars and islands.

The sights and sounds of cranes roosting on the Platte are immeasurably old, but also forever new and variable. Gradually, as twilight descends into night, the noise level of roosting flocks gradually dies down. Yet all night long, some cranes in every flock stand watch while others sleep with bills tucked under their wings, the latter presumably secure in the knowledge that some of their group are always alert and watching for danger.

These unspoken promises, both daily and annual, that the cranes keep with one another and with the river remind us of our individual promises and personal obligations to ourselves, our kin, and our land. Holding the hand of a grandchild as a flock of cranes passes overhead, and telling her that if she is lucky she might also one day show these same sights to her own grandchild, is a powerful lesson in faith, hope, and love. And beauty, touched by love, is somehow transformed into magic.

Our wild cranes also have a powerful attraction that has held me captive for nearly half a century. I have written this book to try help spread some of that magical power to others. I hope my readers will find some of it rubbing off these pages and into their hearts and will join me in helping to protect and preserve the wonderful natural legacies of the cranes and their precious wetlands.

Acknowledgments

It has been nearly two decades since I wrote my last book on cranes (*Crane Music: A Natural History of American Cranes*, 1991), and during that time I have never lost my fascination with these marvelous birds. From the time the sandhill cranes leave Nebraska's Platte River valley each April until I hear their overhead voices again in autumn, the world seems a more somber and less entrancing place. My only consolation then lies in the knowledge that they will return in October and lift my spirits once again, if only until they disappear too quickly, riding a frigid north wind to their traditional wintering grounds. There are now only two seasons in my personal calendar—crane season and the rest of the year.

I decided to write this book for several reasons. First, I still feel an unrelenting need to inform others of the special values and aesthetic appeal of wild cranes. I would far rather see and listen to cranes than gaze once more on Arizona's magnificent Grand Canyon, or listen to a concert performed by the finest of the world's choirs. I can live without both of these; the Grand Canyon's overall appearance hasn't changed an iota during my lifetime, and no mix of human voices can resonate with the beauty, power, and authority of the unique chorus of wild cranes drifting down from a cerulean sky.

Second, my other crane books have become increasingly outdated, especially with regard to recent sandhill and whooping crane population trends. There is now much new information as to the migrations, distributions, and biology of our cranes, and of the ever-changing threats to their long-term survival. After nearly a half-century of experiencing cranes, I feel it my duty to document these important aspects of their biology and ecology one more time, rather than going quietly into that good night of silence.

I also have had increasing forebodings of the ecological consequences of global warming and expanding human population pressures, and their effects on our dwindling water resources and wetland habitats. Nearly all the world's cranes have populations that are declining, threatened, or endangered. Our native whooping crane has been in that last sad category for my entire lifetime, and its long-term survival still remains precarious.

I have had much help over the years in continuing to fuel my obsession with cranes. The staff of Audubon's Rowe Sanctuary along Nebraska's Platte River, and especially Rowe's past director Paul Tebble, always welcomed me and allowed me to use their blinds, as did the staffs of Crane Meadows Nature Center, the Platte River Whooping Crane Maintenance Trust, and the Nature Conservancy. The first time I entered a crane blind was in 1970, with my one-time student Tom Mangelsen who, like me, has never wavered in his love for cranes or his commitment to their conservation. Since then, no spring has been complete unless we have watched cranes together beside the Platte River.

Various friends have encouraged me to transfer my thoughts to paper, such as JoD Blessing and Amy Richert, who both would agree that wild cranes are far more than

mere birds, and instead approach the realm of magic. James Harris of the International Crane Foundation critiqued an early partial draft, and George Archibald offered several helpful ideas, including suggesting the book's title. I also benefited from assistance from the staff of the International Crane Foundation, especially xix
Jeb Barzen, Betsy Didrickson, Anne Lacey, and Sara Zimorski.

Parts or all of the manuscript were read at various stages and critiqued by Linda Brown, Karine Gil-Weir, Amy Richert, and Barbara Voeltz. Eric Volden helped me write site descriptions for some birding locations in Nebraska's Rainwater Basin. Information on other locations was provided by Christian Artuso, Hugh Boyd, Amber Burnette, Jim Duncan, Cheri Gratto-Trevor, Evelyn Horn, Brian Johns, Dan Nieman, Glen Suggett, Peter Taylor, and Gus Yaki.

The ink drawings are all my own. The range maps are derived from those that I originally drew for my 1991 *Crane Music*, but have been updated to show some recent distributional changes and incorporate new information.

Many friends have accompanied me on scores of crane-watching trips, from the tundras of Canada and Alaska to the deserts of Arizona, and have shared in my joys of being in the company of cranes. Names that spring to mind include Linda Brown, Jackie Canterbury, Allison Johnson, Josef Kren, and my numerous ornithology teaching assistants, such as Mary Bomberger, Dan Hatch, Clair Johnson, David Joyner, Myra Niemeier, Roger Sharpe, Jean Tate, and James Tate. There are also the hundreds of ornithology students with whom I have shared the wonders of the Platte Valley in spring, and who rarely complained about getting wet, cold, or hungry (except for one unfortunate person who was inadvertently left on the river and had to hitchhike home). To all I offer my thanks for the rich memories they evoke. And, most of all, I must thank the cranes for simply being there.

xx

All royalties from this book have been assigned to Nebraska's Lillian Annette Rowe Sanctuary and Iain Audubon Center, in honor of their unflagging efforts to preserve our priceless cranes and other vulnerable wildlife, as well as our increasingly threatened Platte River.

Sandhill and Whooping Cranes

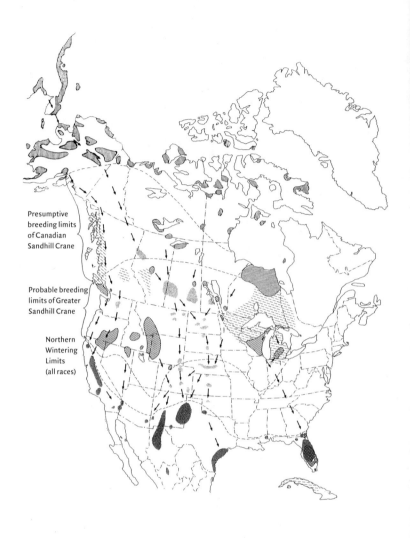

Presumptive
breeding limits
of Canadian
Sandhill Crane

Probable breeding
limits of Greater
Sandhill Crane

Northern
Wintering
Limits
(all races)

MAP 1. Breeding ranges of the lesser (vertical hatching), Canadian (horizontal hatching) and greater (diagonal hatching) sandhill cranes, and residential distributions of the Mississippi and Florida sandhill cranes (cross-hatching). Broken hatching indicates breeding areas not shown on the map in *Crane Music* (Johnsgard 1991), plus the residential range of the Cuban sandhill crane. Adapted from Johnsgard (1991).

One. Lesser Sandhill Cranes

Pleistocene Relics from the Tundra

There is a wonderful old tradition in some parts of Scandinavia, in which the children hang their stockings outside their houses during those days in early spring when the European common cranes first return from their wintering areas in France and Spain. Sometimes the children place an ear of corn or some other gift for the cranes, whose welcome voices and overhead flocks are the surest sign of spring and renewed hope for the future after enduring a long, unbearably dark and frigid Scandinavian winter.

Spring in the northern latitudes is an auspicious time to be alive—a time above all to watch birds—the word auspicious is of pre-Christian origin (from the Latin), meaning to divine the future by watching the movements of birds.

Each spring the arc of the sun swings slowly northward until it reaches the vernal equinox in late March. Then for a singular day it rises above the horizon at exactly due east, and also sets precisely twelve hours later at due west. At such times I am reminded of Eos, Greek goddess of the dawn, her pre-sunrise presence projected above the eastern horizon as pinkish fingers of radiant light. We have a collective cultural memory of her to thank for the Old English word "east," meaning the direction of sunrise. Indeed we must also thank Eos for the idea of Easter itself, which was once a pagan celebration of the annual vernal return of the sun, and of the inevitable victory of spring's renewal over the long darkness of winter.

And so I turn my eyes toward the east each spring, making sure that I am witness to at least one sunrise and sunset in the company of migrating birds. Most often it is shared with sandhill cranes gathering in the Platte Valley, but occasionally with migrating wildfowl that are also stirred to move northward, following the northward sweep of the sun. In some special places, and at such precious times, it is easy to imagine that one is a part of a different world, where warfare and famine are far removed. There the combined noises of wind, uncounted wings, and a chorus of skyward voices are little if at all different from the sounds that were present during the last ice age of one hundred thousand years ago.

I suspect that the migrating cranes of a pre–ice age period some ten million years ago would fully understand every nuance of the crane conversation going on today along the Platte. Cranes have scarcely changed in the last ten million years, whereas the world around them now would be scarcely recognizable to birds of that era.

Driving west from Lincoln to Grand Island is like driving backward in time. One begins by passing over rolling hills of glacial till, sprinkled with rounded and ice-scarred boulders that were deposited randomly across the landscape as the last glacier retreated about eleven thousand years ago. Within fifty miles the land is flatter, and the wind-carried loess soil underneath the grassy mantle dates back at least a half-million years. The meadowlarks singing here from the fence posts are all westerns, the easterns being seemingly unable or unwilling to leave their familiar patches of remnant tallgrass prairie to the east. Great flocks of blackbirds move like dust clouds though the sky, sometimes briefly stopping to decorate leaf-bare trees, then moving on like restless spirits searching endlessly for suitable final resting places. Red-tailed hawks soar lazily above, their wingtips delicately seeking out the faint updrafts coming from the sun-warmed earth, and their circling paths reminding one that all of life consists of repeated cycles, and that the earth's orbit has gone full circle one more time since their return the previous spring.

3

At times like this, one can only pity most Americans, who have never known the special thrill of sitting quietly among streamside prairie grasses, as the returning cranes alight and perform their nightly rituals with the river, and the river in return offers its own quiet nightly sanctuary to the weary birds. It is an appropriate time and place to worship the earth and all its manifold beauties, and especially to give thanks to Eos, or whatever other god or goddess one happens personally to worship, for being able to experience another Platte River spring.

Early March is a time in Nebraska when the natural world changes on an almost day-to-day basis, with spring arriving in erratic fits and starts, as bone-chilling north and welcome south winds blow across the plains in regular alternation. Nevertheless, day lengths during early March are increasing at a nearly perceptible rate, and the sunrises and sunsets creep ever closer toward marking exact eastern and western compass points on the horizon.

For naturalists, March is a time for rejoicing, for on its soothing south winds sweep wave after wave of northbound migrant birds. By the first of March the Platte River has usually fully thawed, although thin ice shelves might line its edges on frosty mornings, and dying snow patches are usually confined to deeper ditches and the shady sides of buildings.

In towns and cities, cardinals have already been singing enthusiastically from trees for nearly two months. Northbound sparrows and horned larks are now abandoning their winter foraging grounds in weedy edges, stubble, and ploughed fields, and are disappearing from view, only to be replaced quickly by countless red-winged blackbirds.

As recently as forty years ago, the first of March represented the average arrival date for sandhill cranes at the Platte River. Recent warmer winters and earlier thaws have tended to shift their first arrival date back into late or even mid-February, the birds being driven ever northward by a combination of hormones, experience, and melting ice. Thus by the middle of February there are now usually a few flocks of cranes braving the possibility of late blizzards and icy Platte River waters, giving them early opportunities at the waste grain scattered across the harvested cornfields of the Platte Valley, from Grand Island west to Scottsbluff.

The sandhill cranes arrive in the Platte Valley none too soon. By the time they arrive, vast flocks of cold-tolerant snow geese are already present, and thousands of overwintering Canada geese are consuming waste corn from fields all along the central and western Platte Valley. Overwintering by Canada geese in the Platte Valley has greatly increased in recent decades, so that tens of thousands of birds now often sit out the winter here, rather than pushing farther south. The snow goose flocks that now number close to two million and that once migrated northward along the Missouri valley

1. Adult lesser sandhill cranes descending

have shifted westward to the Platte Valley during the past few decades, probably because of greater corn-foraging opportunities here. Scattered among the snow geese, and comprising about 2 percent of the flocks, are the nearly identical Ross's geese, miniature versions of snow geese that are also headed toward high-arctic nesting grounds.

Adding to these are multitudes of the tens of thousands of cackling geese and the probably larger numbers of greater white-fronted geese staging in the Platte, and the March goose population in the Platte Valley and adjoining Rainwater Basin to the south may easily reach or exceed three million birds. And, adding to the mix, mallards and northern pintails are the vanguards of a dozen or more species of ducks that pour into the Platte Valley and Rainwater Basin during early March. All in all, it is an avian spectacle possibly unmatched anywhere in North America, with perhaps nearly ten million waterfowl and up to almost half a million sand-hill cranes concentrating in the Platte Valley at peak numbers.

And, if rarity, rather than uncountable numbers, is the naturalist's goal, then the possibility also exists of seeing a few whooping cranes, one of North America's rarest and most beautiful birds. Probably all of the Great Plains flock of whooping cranes, which now numbers nearly three hundred birds, passes through Nebraska each spring. However, whooping cranes tend to arrive later in spring than do the sandhill cranes, and very few are likely to appear before the first of April. They also migrate in small, often family-sized, groups and, to avoid unnecessary (and illegal) disturbance and harassment, their exact stopping points are never publicized by state and federal agencies. As a result, its takes great luck to encounter any whooping cranes in the state.

Even rarer than the whooping crane is the Eurasian or common crane, the universally cherished crane of European myth and folklore, which has been reported in North America less than a dozen times. Most of these sightings have occurred in Nebraska's Platte Valley, where the birds have unexpectedly appeared among flocks of sandhill cranes. Probably these birds headed east, rather than turning south, on reaching the Bering Strait during fall migration out of Siberia, and followed sandhill cranes to their wintering areas.

Unlike waterfowl and songbirds, which often migrate at night, cranes are daylight migrants, mainly because they rely on their soaring ability to carry them from point to point. By using thermal updrafts, which develop during warm days as sun-warmed air rises from the ground, the birds can ascend thousands of feet with little physical effort, and then glide on a slight downward flight path for many miles, until they locate another thermal. Migration is most often done during times of excellent visibility and favorable tailwinds; strong crosswinds may cause them to drift off course. Only rarely do cranes attempt to migrate at night, perhaps with the help of a full moon.

At a flight speed of forty-five to fifty miles per hour, sandhill cranes can cover up to about five hundred miles in a single day, or nearly all the way from their Texas and New Mexico wintering grounds to the Platte Valley. However, brief stopovers at refuges such as Salt Plains or Quivira in Oklahoma, or Cheyenne Bottoms in Kansas, are not rare. It is a great joy to be watching and waiting along the Platte after a warm March day, and

2. Lesser sandhill cranes landing in the Platte River

to hear the clarion calls of arriving cranes thousands of feet above. As they recognize their long-remembered roosting sites on the Platte, the flock begins a lazy, circling glide downward to land among its protective sandbars and islands.

For the sandhill cranes, the Platte River offers safe 9 nighttime roosting sites on sandy islands and bars. During the daylight hours, from about sunrise until sunset, the birds spend their time in harvested cornfields and wet meadows, eating predominately corn, which is rapidly converted to fat stores needed for completing the long migration to arctic tundra. A small percentage of their Platte Valley food consists of various invertebrates such as snails and earthworms, providing the protein and calcium that will be needed for egg-laying and other aspects of reproduction.

The first two weeks of March are the peak of goose migration in the Platte Valley, and by then the sandhill crane migration is nearing its peak. This is the ideal time for venturing to the area between Grand Island and Kearney, the focal point of goose and crane concentrations.

During the day, motorists may watch cranes feeding in fields near the river, and revel in the countless skeins of geese and ducks passing overhead, spread out from horizon to horizon, like animated strings of Christmas decorations. Throughout the day, the sounds of crane music drift down from the sky, as the birds move from field to field, or back toward the river after eating their fill.

I once thought the music of cranes perhaps most comparable to that of angels singing, but on further thought I believe that this is an unfair comparison.

Angel choruses, judging from the paintings one sees, seem to be highly biased in favor of young, nubile females, whereas the music of crane flocks exhibits all the democratic exuberance imaginable when every bird, regardless of sex and age, is calling simultaneously at full voice, regardless of pitch. Crane chorusing can only remind one of listening to an amateur performance of Handel's "Hallelujah Chorus" as chaotically sung by a vast assemblage of tone-deaf but enthusiastic lovers of fine music.

As spring moves forward in eastern Nebraska, with the first redbud blossoms bursting tentatively into bloom, I know I must return to the Platte one last time to bid farewell to the cranes. One recent Easter weekend in early April seemed a perfect choice for this sad delight. A strong, persistent south wind the previous week had blown the snow geese northward toward the edges of their own known world, and I also knew that the cranes wouldn't be able to resist the urge to leave the Platte Valley much longer. The moon was ripening to its monthly fullness, and owls were starting to appear at twilight, hunting for mice to feed their growing broods of young. A few nights previously I had watched entranced, as male woodcocks did their graceful sky dances by moonlight, while small and nearly invisible flocks of ducks sliced noisily through a star-studded sky.

Arriving at the Platte, I found its channels to be narrower and shallower than they had been only a few weeks before, a sign that irrigation upstream had begun. The snow, Ross's, cackling, and white-fronted geese were now all gone, and blue-winged teal puddled busily in roadside ditches and ponds where scaup, buffleheads, and goldeneyes had courted enthusiastically barely a month before. Search as I might, there were only a few scattered pairs of cranes to be seen. At least some of these seemed to consist of pairs with one of their members disabled and unable to continue the long trek northward. Clearly I had just missed the great exodus of birds; a few somber gray feathers caught up in shoreline vegetation gave testimony to their owners' recent departure. 11

Searching the northern horizon, I could see nothing but blue sky and large cumulus clouds. These offered strong visual evidence that this was a good day for riding on the strong thermal updrafts developing below the cottony white clouds. I could only wish the birds a silent but heartfelt Godspeed, and hope that most of them would again decorate the skies of Nebraska in five or six months.

In the last few years, much has been learned of the northward migrations of the lesser sandhills that visit the Platte Valley. Most of this information is derived from the work of Jane Austin, Douglas Johnson, Gary Krapu, and other biologists from the Northern Prairie Wildlife Research Station in North Dakota. By trapping, banding, and placing small (one-ounce) transmitters on northward-bound cranes, their movements have been able to be tracked by satellites. As a result, the major migration routes and breeding areas of the birds have been determined.

In general, the sandhills that stage along the eastern end of the Platte's riparian roosting habitat (which extends east to Grand Island) migrate in a north to northeasterly direction, breeding north to the Hudson Bay region and northeastern Canada. The largest birds may be found from the vicinity of Grand Island to the vicinity of Shelton, about twenty-five miles west, and approach the size range of greater sandhill cranes. In the spring, greater sandhill cranes typically weigh more than ten pounds, and their beak lengths average about 40 percent longer than those of lesser sandhill cranes. The nearest breeding grounds of greater sandhill cranes are in Minnesota, so it is not surprising that a few might pause at the easternmost edge of the central Platte Valley.

Those sandhills that concentrate in the middle portions of the Platte Valley during March begin to move north and spread out widely after they migrate out of the valley in April, headed for breeding grounds in the subarctic boreal forests and parkland regions of Canada. These birds typically weigh seven to eight pounds during their spring stopover period, and are considered to represent the Canadian race of sandhill crane.

The cranes that historically and to a degree still stage in the western part of the North Platte Valley (west locally to Lake McConaughy and even to the vicinity of Scottsbluff) migrate north to arctic tundra breeding regions as remote as Siberia to the west and Canada's Baffin Island to the east. Between 2002 and 2009, the timing of the peak numbers of cranes on the Platte has varied from as early as March 17 to as late as April 8, with an average of March 27 (Karine Gil, personal communication). There is typically a massive departure that often occurs during the first week or two of April. Some of the lesser sandhill cranes fly almost directly north to breeding grounds along Canada's arctic coast, and a few even reach high-arctic islands in central Canada, such as Victoria and Banks islands.

Those cranes bound for Baffin Island should benefit

3. Adult lesser sandhill cranes taking flight

from the establishment of three new National Wildlife Areas in northeastern Baffin Island, including coastal tundra habitats at Isabella Bay and Reid Bay. These new National Wildlife Areas total more than 160,000 square miles, an area greater than Nebraska and Kansas combined.

14

Still other lesser sandhill cranes, probably the majority, gradually veer northwesterly toward northern and western coastal Alaska and northeastern Siberia. These are the smallest of all sandhill cranes, and the ones undertaking the longest migrations. An apparently increasing percentage of these westernmost breeders now stage in the central Platte Valley rather than in their historical areas along the North Platte River. This population shift has probably resulted from the loss of suitable roosting habitat in the North Platte Valley, mostly as a result of dewatering and associated filling in of shorelines, bars, and islands with vegetation, and a subsequent downstream movement of birds into the central Platte Valley. There extensive habitat restoration has restored many of the overgrown bars and islands to their early-succession condition of nearly bare sand substrates, which are ideal for crane roosting (Faanes and LeValley 1993). These islands and bars were historically swept clean of vegetation when ice-melt flooding in early spring had a scouring effect on non-woody vegetation, but recent spring flows have been inadequate to produce this effect.

This long-term downstream shifting of the Plate Valley crane population was stimulated in large part because of declining river flows, which once were adequate to scour the islands and bars free of vegetation each spring. As a result the remaining channels have become narrower but deeper, their sediments coarser, and accompanied by a reduction in wet meadows along the river edges (Kinzel, Nelson, and Parker 2005).

Gary Krapu and David Brandt (2009) have named the cranes that probably staged historically in Nebraska's western Platte and North Platte valleys as the "West Alaska–Siberian subpopulation." These birds average less than seven pounds in spring, and have the shortest beak lengths of all sandhill cranes. Most of them winter on saline lakes, playa wetland and salt flats from western Texas westward into eastern New Mexico and southeastern Arizona, and southward across the Chihuahuan Desert in the Mexican states of Chihuahua and Durango. Some also winter southeast to Coahila and Nuevo Leon, and south as far as Zacatecas and San Luis Potosi (Chavez-Ramirez 2005).

Winter populations in New Mexico's Bitter Lake National Wildlife Refuge had peak populations of about fifty-four thousand in the late 1970s, but these declined to less than six thousand by 1989, when corn acreage also declined. Recent increases in corn production have probably been responsible for bringing the numbers of wintering cranes back to more than ten thousand (Montgomery 2008)

Surveys by U.S. Fish and Wildlife Service personnel between 1963 and 1994 indicated that at times more than fifty thousand sandhills then wintered in Mexico (Drewien, Brown, and Benning 1996. The largest numbers were found at Laguna de Babicora, Ascension, and Laguna de los Mexicanos, all located in Chihuahua. Corn and cultivated cereal grains such as oats are probably important winter foods in this region.

In January of 2009, I visited one of the wintering

grounds of this subpopulation in southeastern Arizona, south of Willcox. This region, the Sulfur Springs Valley, supported up to about 35,000 lesser sandhills in January. Many typically concentrate near Willcox on the Willcox Playa, but even larger numbers can often be seen at Whitewater Draw, between Bisbee and Elfrida. The Arizona Game and Fish Department manages both areas, and both are open for public viewing throughout the winter crane season. Unlike the situation in Nebraska's Platte Valley, where the cranes leave the river at sunrise and do not return until sunset, in these desert areas there are typically two flights a day. The first is at sunrise, when the birds leave the playas and fly out to forage in agricultural fields. They return to the playas in late morning, and remain through midday, with a second foraging trip in the late afternoon. They return to the safety of the playa wetlands by sundown, or perhaps later if there is a full moon.

It is about a six-hundred-mile (thousand-kilometer) flight from the northern Mexican wintering areas to the North Platte Valley, which typically occurs in late February and may be accomplished over a period of several days. These birds typically leave the North Platte Valley in early April, at the same time as those that stage farther east in the central Platte Valley also leave. From the North Platte Valley the western subpopulation flock moves rapidly north to southwestern Saskatchewan, where they may again rest and forage for up to about three weeks.

Then, as weather allows, the birds cross from the Yukon Territory into western Alaska, and follow the Yukon River past Fairbanks, where they soon enter the vast Yukon-Kuskokwim delta region of coastal Alaska.

There many of them join tundra swans, emperor geese, brant, spectacled eiders, and other arctic-nesting waterfowl in one of the greatest wetland breeding grounds in North America. Most of the lesser sandhill cranes in existence breed in this seemingly endless mosaic of water and tundra, as well as perhaps a hundred million other birds, and countless clouds of mosquitoes that plague both birds and humans during the all-too-brief summer. The breeding lesser sandhill pairs that I observed there in June of 1964 were highly scattered over the lowland tundra, and barely within earshot of one another. This area is close enough to the Arctic Circle so that by mid-June the constant sunlight allows the birds to remain active throughout the night, and be vigilant for aerial predators such as golden eagles and gyrfalcons, and egg- or chick-stealing arctic foxes.

17

Many of the cranes fly on to cross the Bering Strait and enter Siberia during May. From there they may continue east along coastal Siberian tundra as far as nine hundred miles, and mostly nest within about fifty miles of the coast. Although the Bering Strait is only about sixty miles wide at its narrowest point, the distance from the Yukon-Kuskokwim delta to Siberia's Chukotka Peninsula is over three hundred miles, in a region noted for having some of the worst weather on earth. While standing on St. George Island of the Pribilofs in early June, I once heard migrating sandhill cranes flying too high to be seen. St. George is about two hundred fifty miles from the west coast of Alaska and more than six hundred miles from the nearest Siberian landfall. Cranes have even been seen as far west in Alaska as Adak and Shelmya islands in the farthest Aleutians; Shelmya Island is at least nine hundred miles beyond the tip of the Alaska Peninsula.

4. Adult lesser sandhill crane landing in threat posture

Krapu and Brandt (2008) reported that six telemetry-equipped sandhills migrated from New Mexico and Arizona wintering grounds in early to mid-March. Two of them went to breeding grounds on the Yukon-Kuskokwim delta. The other four telemetry-equipped cranes traveled to the Chukotka Peninsula, the Chaun delta, and the Anadyr delta of Siberia, arriving in mid- to late May. The easternmost known nesting region, the Kolymskaya Plains at the mouth of the Kolyma River, is about five thousand miles away from the population's southernmost wintering grounds. This situation forces them to not only undertake the longest migration of any North American crane, but also to begin fall migration almost immediately after the young of the year have attained an ability to fly, probably at only fifty to sixty days of age.

Added to a thirty-day incubation period, about ninety days are needed for sandhills to complete breeding in a region that may have a frost-free period of only about two months. Young birds fledged too late in the season are likely to lack the stamina and flying skills needed to undertake the fall migration, and may perish along the way. It is interesting that this population is the smallest of all sandhill cranes, and has relatively longer wings than do the larger crane races, as is also true of the smallest and most highly migratory forms of Canada geese.

The fall return migration for the western Alaska–Siberia population is a carbon copy of the spring route, but different staging areas are sometimes used. Making autumn landfall in western Alaska during late August, the Siberian-breeding cranes stop for a few weeks near Fairbanks, joining those that bred locally or in the Yukon-Kuskokwim delta to the west. Up to several thousand congregate at Creamer's Field Migratory Waterfowl Refuge just outside Fairbanks, and in nearby meadows in the Tanana River valley.

The annual Tanana Valley Sandhill Crane Festival celebrates the return of the cranes. When I visited the refuge a few years ago much of interior Alaska was being subjected to massive forest fires, and visibility was greatly reduced. It was a near-magical experience to watch flocks of cranes slowly materialize from the mix of clouds and smoke and join the flocks of cranes and migrating geese already gathered at Creamer's Field.

Those lesser sandhills that breed farther south along Alaska's Bristol Bay, the Alaska Peninsula, and Cook

Inlet represent the Pacific flyway flock, which have a quite different migratory strategy, based on data from birds fitted with satellite transmitters. These birds begin their fall migration in early September, following the coast through the islands and straits of the Alaska panhandle. Probably most stop for a few days at the Yukutat forelands, along the Bering Glacier lowlands, or the Stikine River delta. Many of these also stop over along Alaska's Copper River delta and near Gustavus. Near the Stikine River delta, the population moves inland and passes through British Columbia along the Fraser and Okanagan valleys.

After entering central Washington they often stage around Potholes Reservoir for about a week; up to thirteen thousand birds have been reported at Soap Lake during September. From there they continue south through southeastern Oregon (staging in the Harney and Warner valleys) to wintering areas in California's Central Valley. On average, this 2,200-mile trip is completed in less than a month, so that the birds arrive in California by early October, wintering in the Sacramento–San Joaquin delta region and in Merced County (Petrula and Rothe 2005).

This Pacific coastal population of lesser sandhills has been legally hunted in southeastern Alaska since 1981, but the annual numbers killed there have been so low (from 199 to 856 per year between 1981 and 1992) as to not generate concern as to possible serious effects on the population. Its population in the early 1990s was estimated as at least twenty-five thousand birds, and was considered stable (Tacha, Nesbitt, and Vohs 1994).

Considering the incredible hardships that lesser

sandhill cranes must undergo to complete their epic spring migrations, to raise chicks under the most severe environmental conditions, and to accompany them back to traditional wintering grounds while enduring a threat of gunfire from Alaska to the southern United States or Mexico, one must wonder about the human-   21 ity of people who think that killing cranes can possibly be sporting.

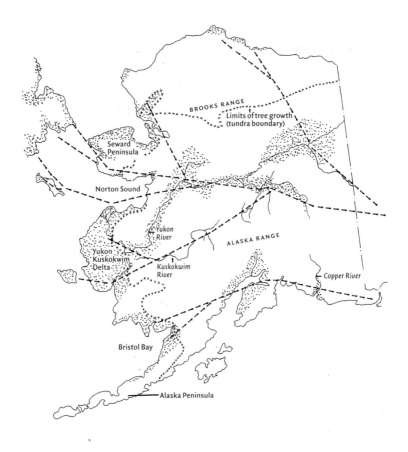

MAP 2. Probable sandhill crane breeding areas (stippling) and fall migration routes (arrows) of sandhill cranes in Alaska and adjacent Siberia. Fall routes drawn in part after Kessel (1984); spring routes are essentially the reverse of those in fall.

Two. The Other Sandhills

From Sedge Bogs to Palm Savannas

The Greater Sandhill Crane

The greater sandhill crane (*Grus canadensis tabida*) has been thriving in recent decades, as a result of generally low hunting rates and effective habitat management on the part of federal, state, and local or private organizations. It consists of three major regional populations.

The Eastern Greater Sandhill Crane

The greater sandhill crane's eastern population, which breeds in the Great Lakes region and migrates to wintering grounds in southern Georgia and Florida, probably now approaches forty thousand birds. This population has increased greatly in recent decades, and has expanded its distribution within the heart of its historic range in Wisconsin and Michigan, as well as reoccupying long-vacated breeding areas such as in Minnesota, Illinois, Indiana, Ohio, Pennsylvania, New York, and Maine.

Sandhill crane numbers in Michigan have increased remarkably in recent decades. Although Michigan's Upper Peninsula has probably always had nesting sandhills, in 1931 there were only seventeen nesting pairs known to be in the Lower Peninsula. By 1947 there still were twenty known Lower Peninsula pairs, and by the 1950s about fifty. A 1986–87 survey reported 650 pairs in the Lower Peninsula, plus at least 175 pairs in the Upper Peninsula. More recent estimates put the

Michigan population (including non-breeders) at more than eight thousand birds.

Local breeding has also extended south from southern Wisconsin, and cranes have begun to nest in northern Illinois (since 1979), northern Indiana (1982), northern Ohio (1985), eastern Iowa (1992), western Pennsylvania (1994), Maine (2000), New York (2003), and Vermont (2007). By the year 2000, thirty or more pairs were nesting in northern Indiana. The Ohio population has also expanded considerably. Between 1997 and 2005 there were at least fifty-eight nestings in that state, and by 2008 there were twenty-four nesting pairs. The largest number of breedings has occurred in Wayne County, and many breeding or non-breeding birds have also been seen in Mercer, Pickaway, Turnbull and Williams counties.

Sandhill cranes historically bred in southern Ontario as well as western Quebec, and recent breedings in western, southwestern, and central Quebec (Letourneau and Morrier 1993) suggest that this historic range is now being reoccupied. Likewise, that part of southeastern Ontario located between James Bay and the Great Lakes has had numerous nesting since the 1980s, geographically connecting the presumed breeding ranges of the greater and Canadian races.

In Wisconsin, an estimated twenty-five pairs of sandhill cranes were present during the 1930s. They have increased markedly in both population size and breeding distribution since then, and especially since the 1980s. Since 1976, volunteers have performed an Annual Midwest Crane Count during mid-April. Initiated in Wisconsin as a single-county survey, it gradually expanded under the direction of the International

Crane Foundation to include all of Wisconsin by 1985, when over six thousand cranes were counted. Parts of Michigan and Minnesota were added to the survey in 1994, plus part of Illinois in 1995, and part of Iowa in 1996.

During the counts of the mid-1990s the highest Wis- consin densities were found in Marquette and Green Lake counties. The count for the year 2000 indicated more than thirteen thousand cranes were then present in Wisconsin. Recent surveys have indicated that a majority of the population occurs in a region roughly bounded by Waushara and Winnebago counties in the north, and by Dane and Jefferson counties in the south. The 2007 annual crane count showed the highest local counts still farther south in Rock County, but with locally large numbers also present in Dane and Columbia counties.

As recently as the 1970s Minnesota's sandhill cranes nested primarily in northwestern parts of the state, with only scattered records from the central region. However, their nesting range has expanded to include central and southeastern Minnesota. The population breeding in northwestern Minnesota and nearby parts of southern Manitoba (the Interlake region north of Winnipeg) and southwestern Ontario consists of perhaps ten to fifteen thousand birds. Unlike the other Minnesota sandhills that migrate southeastwardly, these birds fly directly south to winter on the coast of Texas, where they mingle with Canadian and lesser sandhill cranes, and are exposed to significant sport hunting. At least some of them stage in the eastern Platte Valley during spring, accounting for the very large sandhills that are often seen near Grand Island.

5. Adult greater sandhill crane calling

There have been several recent nestings of sandhill cranes in Iowa, where the last historic records occurred in the 1890s. Starting in 1992 a pair of sandhills began nesting at Otter Creek Marsh, Tama County, central Iowa, and nests have been documented there almost annually since then. Other nestings have occurred in Allamakee, Boone, Bremer, and Woodbury counties.

27

North Dakota's breeding population of greater sandhills declined rapidly during the late nineteenth century and early twentieth century, and the last known nesting occurred in 1916. However, in June of 1974 a family was observed at J. Clark Salyer National Wildlife Refuge, along the Souris River of northern North Dakota. There are no recent nesting records for South Dakota, although nesting once occurred in the Black Hills. The last documented South Dakota breeding (in Sanborn County) was in 1910, but sandhills reportedly nested in South Dakota during 2008 (George Archibald, personal communication).

Historic breeding in the Sandhills region of Nebraska is poorly documented, but certainly occurred as late as the 1880s in Cherry and Holt counties. No twentieth-century breeding records were known for the state until 1999, when a family was discovered near Harvard, Clay County, in the eastern Rainwater Basin. Later breedings have been documented for Clay and Fillmore counties, also in the eastern Rainwater Basin. Successful nesting was documented for at least four successive years (2005–8) on a saline wetland near Bayard, Morrill County, in the western Rainwater Basin. Nesting by a pair also occurred in 2006 and 2008 in Rock County, north-central Nebraska, and two possible nestings occurred in Garfield County in 2007.

All of these recent records suggest that the greater sandhill crane is slowly reclaiming much of its historic breeding range in the upper Great Plains and Great Lakes regions. Most of the records are from state-owned and federally owned properties, as few privately owned sites are large enough to offer the degree of security and privacy needed for cranes to breed successfully.

28

Dense breeding populations place territorial acquisition and maintenance at a premium. In a dense Wisconsin population, it has been found that fifty of seventy breeding pairs switched mates over a fourteen-year period, with forty-five of the pairs switching permanently. Most of the permanent switches followed the death or disappearance of a mate, but some cases of divorce did occur. Evidently the ability to maintain a desirable breeding territory may take precedence over past reproductive success or failure in influencing the probability of divorce. If a nearby territory becomes available, a paired crane may elect to choose another mate, perhaps thereby increasing its reproductive success (Hayes, Barzen and Britten 2008).

Similarly, in dense populations extra-pair paternity may be more likely to occur than in sparse ones. In a different Wisconsin study (Hayes, Britten and Barzen 2008), the measured frequency of extra-pair paternity ranged from 4.4–11 percent over a twelve-year period, based on genetic analyses of progeny. These cases may have resulted from actual infidelity, or perhaps from mate switching prior to genetic testing.

All told, the eastern population of greater sandhill cranes is doing extremely well, thanks in part to a universally high level of population protection. There is still an abundance of potential but unoccupied breeding

6. Adult greater sandhill crane incubating

habitats scattered across southern Canada and the
northeastern United States, providing hopes for future
population expansion. Wintering areas are still plenti-
ful, and the eastern population birds are increasingly
wintering along the Gulf Coast and South Atlantic states
in addition to their historic Florida range.

The Rocky Mountain Greater Sandhill Crane

The Rocky Mountain greater sandhill crane population
breeds from northwestern Montana south into eastern
Idaho, northern Utah, western Wyoming, and western
Colorado. The region's largest breeding concentration
is in eastern Idaho, at Grays Lake National Wildlife
Refuge. There two hundred or more pairs have been
known to nest, and up to twelve hundred individuals
may occur during migration. Their breeding range in
Utah appears to be expanding, and known migration
corridors include Cache and Heber valleys, as well as
the Uintah Basin of northeastern Utah. Greater sandhill
cranes are considered state-threatened in Colorado,
where in 1991 there were an estimated 118 active nest

7. Greater sandhill crane chick and hatching egg

sites (Renner, Gray and Graham 1991). Most recent nestings have occurred in Routt and Moffat counties, but a few have been found in Rio Blanco, Jackson, and Grand counties (Kingery 1998). The sandhill crane is listed as a species of special concern in Wyoming, with most known breeding occurring within and around the Greater Yellowstone Ecosystem.

The Rocky Mountain population was estimated at 20,000–21,500 birds during the early 1990s by Drewien, Brown, and Kendall (1995), and was judged by them to be stable or slightly declining.

During fall migration the San Luis Valley of southern Colorado is a major staging area for this population, and some staging also occurs near Hayden, in Routt County, northwestern Colorado. Aerial surveys and ground counts in the San Luis Valley between 1984 and 1995 averaged about 19,200 birds identified as Rocky Mountain greaters. Some lessers also occurred in this staging area (an estimated 6–26 percent of the total crane population), and a substantial percentage (26 percent) had mid-toe track measurements overlapping those of Canadian and greater sandhill cranes (Benning et al. 1997).

This population winters in central and southern New Mexico and southeastern Arizona. During the spring migration north the flock again stages in the San Luis Valley for a few days. Between 1986 and 1993 an average of 10,656 cranes stopped there in March or early April. When crossing the Divide the birds attain altitudes of about eleven to twelve thousand feet (Benning et al. 1997), making this one of the highest crane migration routes in North America. After crossing the Divide most or all of these cranes stop to rest for

8. Adult greater sandhill crane leading well-grown chick

a time around Fruit Growers Reservoir near Delta, in Colorado's Hart's Basin. They then begin to disperse into breeding areas from western Colorado northwest to Wyoming, Idaho, and Montana.

A relatively small population of greater sandhills breeds in northeastern Nevada, mostly in Elko and White Pine counties, and adjacent southwestern Idaho. These birds stage in autumn in the White River valley near Lund, Nevada, then continue south to winter along Arizona's Lower Colorado and Gila rivers, and in California's Imperial Valley. The Imperial National Wildlife Refuge provides winter crane habitat on the California side of the Colorado River. On the Arizona side many cranes winter at Cibola National Wildlife Refuge, in the Colorado River Indian Reservation, and on the Gila River below Gillespie Dam. About twenty-five hundred birds were wintering in the Lower Colorado River valley by 2005, and the population had been slowly increasing.

Arizona began a limited hunting season on greater sandhill cranes in 1981, and was later successively joined by Wyoming, New Mexico, Utah, Montana, and Idaho. 33 Annual fall recruitment rates of the Rocky Mountain population over a twenty-one-year period ending in the early 1990s averaged 8.1 percent, and annual survival rates ranged from 91–95 percent during that period (Drewien, Brown and Kendall 1995). For the approximately three-decade period 1972–2005 the estimated annual recruitment for the population, based on fall counts in the San Luis Valley of Colorado, averaged 7.2 percent (Kruse, Sharp and Dubovsky 2008). These are substantially lower recruitment rates than the 9.3–14.3 percent rates reported for the eastern population of greaters (Drewien, Brown, and Kendall 1995).

Drewien, Brown, and Kendall (1995) concluded from their recruitment and mortality data that the Rocky Mountain population could not sustain any increased harvests. The average retrieved kill from 1990 through 1994 was 406 birds. However, by 2002 about six hundred to eight hundred cranes were annually being killed for sport.

The Pacific Greater Sandhill Crane

There is also a Pacific flyway population of greater sandhills breeding from southern British Columbia south to northeastern California (south to Sierra County), and wintering in California's Central and Imperial valleys. California's breeding population is fairly small, but appears to have been increasing. For example, the

2000 breeding population estimate for northeastern California totaled 465 pairs, up from 112 pairs in 1971 (Schlorff 2005).

The largest component of this population (the "Central Valley Population") breeds in eastern Oregon. It numbered about two thousand breeders in the early 1990s, and was centered in the Harney Basin. The highest concentrations occur at Malheur National Wildlife Refuge, which at times has supported more than two hundred nesting pairs.

The remaining parts of this western population are scattered from southern Washington (twenty-three breeding pairs in 2007, nesting in Yakima and Klickitat counties, mainly in Glenwood Valley) north into interior British Columbia. There they breed in the Kamloops area and extend northward in the Cariboo region between the Fraser and North Thompson rivers, at least to the vicinity of Quesnel Lake, judging from preliminary data being gathered for the forthcoming *British Columbia Breeding Bird Atlas.* It is probable that these birds are greaters (Cooper 1996), but they might grade into the slightly smaller Canadian race still farther north. Their migration route is still unstudied, but in spring they may follow the Okanagan valley north from Washington, as crane flocks of unknowns have been reported in April near Okanagan Falls.

Probably almost all of the Pacific flyway greaters winter in California, but their numbers there are hard to estimate, since an unknown number of Canadian sandhill cranes also winter in California. Additionally, many of the estimated twenty to twenty-three thousand lesser sandhills that breed around Alaska's Cook Inlet and Bristol Bay winter in California's Sacramento–San

Joaquin River delta and in Merced County (Petrula and Rothe 2005), making inventories of greaters even more difficult.

Gary Ivey and Caroline Herzinger (2008) reported that about fifteen hundred greater sandhills winter at Staten Island, a Nature Conservancy property in the Sacramento–San Joaquin delta, and that this site represented 36 percent of all crane foraging activity in that region. Winter counts of all-sized cranes in the delta made by Ronald Schorff (2005) in 2000–2001 totaled six thousand to fourteen thousand birds, of which a substantial proportion might have been greaters.

Earlier studies during the mid-1980s by Tom Pogson and Susan Lindstedt (1991) indicated that six thousand to sixty-eight hundred large cranes then wintered between Chico (Butte County) and Pixley National Wildlife Refuge (Tulare County), with 95 percent of them concentrated in the Sacramento valley and the northeastern delta region. These authors judged that the majority of these birds had originated in coastal or interior British Columbia, which would mean they might be a mixture of greater and Canadian sandhills.

At the southern end of California's Central Valley, peak numbers of about fourteen thousand sandhills have developed during November along the San Joaquin River at San Luis National Wildlife Refuge, and about six thousand at Pixley National Wildlife Refuge. It seems possible that these southern wintering groups may have a predominance of the smaller and more highly migratory crane populations.

In the absence of more precise information, a very tentative estimate of six thousand to seven thousand greater sandhill cranes in the Pacific flyway during recent years might seem reasonable, or perhaps nearly double that number if presumptive Canadian sandhills are included.

The Canadian Sandhill Crane

36   The Canadian race of sandhill crane (*G. c. rowani*) was not described until Lawrence Walkinshaw (1965) reported that cranes of intermediate size between greaters and lessers occur across a broad section of central Canada. He judged that they might breed from British Columbia east to northern Ontario, but the population's indefinite size limits made it impossible to define the race's breeding range more precisely. Later John Aldrich (1979) examined over four hundred specimens and judged that their breeding range extended from south-central MacKenzie District of the Northwest Territories east to northern Ontario and James Bay, in aspen parklands and boreal coniferous forest wetlands.

Genetic studies show no apparent separations of sandhill crane populations into three recognizable types. Instead there is a gradual or unbroken clinal gradient from the smallest arctic-breeding lessers through intermediate-sized Canadians to the largest temperate-breeding greaters (Tacha, Vohs, and Ward 1985; Rhymer et al. 2001; Glenn et al. 2002; Peterson et al. 2003). When only two subspecies are recognized, the intermediate-sized birds are merged with greaters.

Douglas Johnson, Jane Austin, and Jill Shaffer (2005) have reviewed the morphological evidence for the recognition of the Canadian race, and found it to be separable on that basis, in spite of a general size gradient from the largest to smallest birds. Based on nearly fifty intermediate-sized specimens examined by them, the summer range of this subarctic and boreal forest population extends at least as far east as James Bay in eastern Ontario. From eastern Ontario it extends north to western Hudson Bay (the vicinity of Churchill, Manitoba), west at least to the Rocky Mountains of western Alberta, and northwest to at least the vicinity of Great Slave Lake in the Northwest Territories.

Cranes from Canadian breeding grounds considered by Johnson et al. (2005) to be of the Canadian race had beak (culmen) and tarsal lengths that averaged (sexes combined) 90 percent those of greaters. Wing (chord) measurements were very similar, averaging 92 percent those of greaters.

Comparing the beak and tarsal lengths of lesser sandhills with greaters, those of lessers respectively averaged 72 percent and 74 percent as long as greaters. However, wing (chord) lengths averaged 87 percent those of greaters. In a larger sample incorporating several studies (Schmitt and Hale 1997), the beak and tarsal percentages respectively averaged about 71 and 78 percent those of greaters, while the wing measurements averaged about 88 percent as long. The relatively long wings of lesser sandhill cranes probably reflect an adaptation to their very long migration routes as compared with greaters.

Not many weights of Canadian sandhill cranes are available, but John Lewis (1979b) reported that adult females from Nebraska averaged 8.31 pounds (3.77 kilograms) and males 8.97 pounds (4.08 kilograms).

Gary Krapu and others (2005) reported that Platte Valley cranes that they identified as female lessers averaged from about 7.3–7.55) pounds (3.3–3.4 kilograms) during spring, and males about 7.5–7.7 pounds (3.4–3.6

kilograms). Earlier, John Lewis (1979) had reported that female lessers from Nebraska similarly (7.38 pounds (averaged 3.35 kilograms) and males (8.24 pounds (3.75 kilograms). Not surprisingly, weights of lessers shot in New Mexico during winter averaged slightly less than these (Schmitt and Hale 1997).

38

Krapu et al. (2005) did not recognize the Canadian race, and those birds that they identified as greaters in Nebraska averaged about 8.9–9.8 pounds (4.0–4.4 kilograms) among females, and about 8.95–9.4 pounds (4.1–4.3 kilograms) among males.

Northern Ontario may represent an important breeding region for the Canadian sandhill crane. It is therefore significant that the Canadian government recently established a massive wildlife protection area in northern Ontario totaling more than eighty thousand square miles (225,000 square kilometers), a region equal to 43 percent of the province's total land mass, and larger than the entire state of Nebraska.

The probable breeding range of the Canadian sandhill crane includes northwestern Manitoba and extends west through Saskatchewan (south to the Qu'Apple valley of southeastern Saskatchewan) and most of northern and central Alberta. Previously known to breed south only to Alberta's Rocky Mountain House, sandhill cranes are now known to nest south to at least Bottrell. The highest incidence of abundance occurs across the Canadian Shield, followed by the Rocky Mountain foothills and the boreal forest natural regions (Semenchuk 1992).

This race evidently also breeds west of the Rocky Mountains to the Pacific Coast, since recent studies suggest that those sandhill cranes nesting on coastal islands in southeastern Alaska (Dall and Prince of Wales islands) and British Columbia are also probably part of the Canadian subspecies (Littlefield and Ivey 2002). The population of cranes nesting along the central and northern British Columbian coast and its coastal islands may number about four thousand birds. Known coastal nesting areas include the Queen Charlotte Islands (Haida Gwaii) and northern Vancouver Island (Godfrey 1986; Cooper 1996). Birds of this intermediate-size class may also extend north to Alaska's Copper River delta (Herter 1982), or at least to the vicinity of Juneau, where cranes have been reported during the breeding season.

These birds evidently follow a fall migration route similar to that described for the Pacific flyway population of lesser sandhill cranes. Most winter in California's Central Valley (Petrula and Rothe 2005), although up to a thousand may overwinter along the lower Columbia River, Clark and Cowlitz counties, Washington (Littlefield and Ivey 2002).

The only known important staging area between their Alaskan and British Columbian breeding grounds and their California wintering grounds is the lower Columbia River region, especially at Sauvie Island Wildlife Management Area, Oregon, and Ridgefield National Wildlife Refuge, Washington. Recent counts there in early fall have indicated a maximum of about four thousand birds (Ivey, Herzinger, and Hoffmann 2005), which, in the absence of other information, might offer a very minimum estimate of the Pacific flyway population of Canadian sandhills.

Only a limited amount of information exists on the migrations of Canadian sandhills, but four birds from the boreal forests of east-central Saskatchewan were fitted with satellite-tracking transmitters. Only two could be tracked, but one moved south to a traditional sandhills staging region around Last Mountain, Kutawagan, and the Quill Lakes in central Saskatchewan. At least 40 one spent about two weeks in central North Dakota. Both also had November stopovers in central Kansas, near Quivira National Wildlife Refuge, a major fall staging area for mid-continent sandhill cranes. One of the birds wintered in northern Tamaulipas, nearly two thousand miles from its summer area (Hjertaas et al. 2001).

It appears that central North Dakota may be an important migratory corridor for Canadian sandhill cranes. Data collected from hunter-killed cranes between 1990 and 1994 indicated that 18 percent consisted of greaters, 36 percent of Canadians, and 46 percent of lessers. Lesser sandhills predominated in the more western specimens, such as those from McLean County, while Canadians and greaters were more common farther east, such those from Pierce and Kidder counties (Kendall, Johnson, and Kohn 1997).

Like its uncertain breeding range and migration routes, the overall winter distribution of the Canadian sandhill crane also remains to be established. For example, it is clear that not all Canadian sandhill cranes of the mid-continent population winter along the coast of Texas. Studies of cranes killed in the middle Rio Grande Valley of New Mexico and the lower Rio Grande Valley of southwestern New Mexico between 1982 and 1995 indicate that all three races may occur there during winter (Schmitt and Hale 1997). In the middle Rio Grande Valley (Bosque del Apache area) Canadians comprised 7 percent of the kill, lessers 27 percent, and greaters 67 percent. In the southern Rio Grande Valley (Luna, Sierra, and Dona Ana counties) Canadians comprised 13 percent of the kill, lessers 67 percent, and greaters 20 percent. The near-reversal of lesser and greater percentages over a geographic distance of only a few hundred miles is surprising.

41

Thomas Tacha, Stephen Nesbitt, and Paul Vohs (1994) judged that the segment of sandhill cranes wintering in the Gulf Coast region to number at least thirty thousand birds. Of these, 33 percent (about ten thousand) were judged to be comprised of lessers, nine percent (about three thousand) greaters, and the remaining 58 percent (about seventeen thousand) presumably Canadians. Other size estimates of this population have ranged very widely, from about 13,500 to 166,000 (Johnson and Kendall 1997). Assuming a typical 9 percent crane recruitment rate, it might number about sixty thousand birds.

Tacha, Nesbitt, and Vohs also judged that in the western subpopulation of sandhill cranes (those staging in the North Platte and western Platte Valley and wintering from Central Texas west) about 80 percent were lessers and more than 1 percent were greaters, leaving about 20 percent unspecified. Probably at least some of these would fall into the intermediate size category of Canadians.

Although recent genetic work has cast doubt on the validity of recognizing the Canadian form as taxonomically distinct, these birds obviously differ somewhat from the other sandhills in their breeding range and habitats, and in their migration routes and timing. Thus many field biologists favor a continuing recognition of the Canadian race, at least for management purposes (Ivey, Herzinger, and Hoffmann 2005).

The Florida Sandhill Crane

The Florida race of the sandhill crane is nonmigratory and residential in Florida and Georgia. Recent genetic research indicates that the Florida population evolved from the eastern flyway population of greater sandhill cranes (Jones et al. 2005). Since the late 1970s it has numbered a few thousand birds, all limited to Florida except for a population of about five hundred birds in and near Georgia's Okefenokee Swamp. Studies by Stephen Nesbitt and others (2001) indicate that Florida sandhills exhibit an early sexual maturity, and may attempt to breed when males are as young as two years, and females at three, as compared with the four to five years required for attaining maturity in the migratory populations. The modal age for first successful reproduction in Florida ranged from 3 years (males) to 4.7 years (females). This early development of maturity perhaps reflects the absence of migration-related stresses in this population.

Because of the mild climate in Florida there is a long breeding season of up to nine months. As a reflection of this extended season, as many as three renesting efforts have been observed following nest or brood failure, even in cases where chicks had survived as long at sixteen days. The average post-fledging brood size was 1.27 young (Nesbitt et al. 2001), which is a notably high rearing-success rate for any sandhill crane population. Allen and Laurel Bennett (1990) found that 57 percent of 187 nests in Georgia's Okefenokee Swamp hatched at least one egg, and that most pairs renested following nest failure, resulting in a fairly high nesting success in spite of significant raccoon predation.

Like other sandhill cranes, Florida sandhill cranes sometimes switch mates. Of seventy-two pairs studied, 44 percent switched mates between 1972 and 1992. Of these, 67.7 percent were due to death of a partner, and 32.3 percent a result of divorce. In both greater and Florida sandhill cranes, mate switching is more likely to occur between pairs that failed to reproduce; over half of such pairs divorced, as compared with only 10 percent of those having a history of successful reproduction. In cases of mate switching, males were much more likely to retain the nesting territory than were females. Whereas initial pair-bonding in cranes is a complex and protracted process, new pair bonds following death or divorce typically were formed very rapidly, often within a few days (Nesbitt and Tacha 1997).

A total of forty-two Florida sandhill nests were closely monitored through 1996. Twenty-five of these nests hatched at least one chick, and twenty-one of the thirty-eight chicks that hatched survived to fledging. Predation, mostly by mammals, was the most common cause of chick mortality, with bobcats and coyotes being the most likely causal agents (Nesbitt, Schwikert, and Spalding 2008). Bobcats have also proven to be very serious predators on whooping cranes in Florida.

The annual percentages of juveniles in the Florida population averaged 11.9 percent over seven years, indicating a relatively high reproductive success. Adult annual survival was estimated as 86.7 percent (Nesbitt et al. 2001). This survival rate is similar to that found in other unhunted populations of sandhill cranes (Johnson and Kendall 1997).

All told, these reproduction statistics indicate that this should be a thriving population. Yet, although it has adapted surprisingly well to sometimes almost suburban situations, habitat fragmentation and loss have severely limited the Florida population's potential. There has been an estimated reduction of suitable habitat of nearly 40 percent between 1974 and 2003, and an estimated decline in the population of 33.7 percent between 1974 and 2003. The 2003 estimate of 4,594 birds, including about 2,150 paired adults, suggests that this race may be unable to maintain its range or numbers in the future without a concerted effort to preserve and manage its habitats (Nesbitt and Hatchitt 2008). It is considered threatened in Florida.

The Mississippi Sandhill Crane

The nonmigratory Mississippi and Cuban races of sandhill cranes may be the last remnants of a single population that once extended from Florida to Cuba, and west along the Gulf coast to at least Mississippi. Recent genetic research indicates that the Mississippi sandhill crane population evolved from the mid-continent population of greater sandhill cranes (Jones et al. 2005).

The Mississippi race is federally endangered and confined to a single national wildlife refuge of 19,400 acres, of which only about 12,500 acres are suitable for cranes. Perhaps always fairly small, the total documented Mississippi crane population didn't rise above one hundred birds until the late 1980s.

The Mississippi Sandhill Crane National Wildlife Refuge was established in 1975, when the race was already on the brink of extinction, and numbered fewer than thirty birds. Even after the refuge was established the crane population rose very slowly. Between 2003 and 2005 extensive efforts were made to improve habitat, control predators, and introduce about seventeen to twenty-five captive-reared juveniles into the population annually. During that period twenty-one pairs produced an average of twenty-seven nests annually (including renestings), but fewer than three young were fledged per year. Winter populations during that period ranged from 110 to 125 birds. Hurricane Katrina in August of 2005 also killed those breeding pairs that had produced 40 percent of the young since 1997 (Hereford and Grazia 2008). More recently the population has reached about 130, but has been supplemented by captive-bred birds, since the wild stock has been unable to maintain itself.

45

The Cuban Sandhill Crane

The Cuban sandhill crane is a remnant and endangered population with limited remaining habitats, and in recent decades its numbers have gradually declined. Recent genetic research indicates that the Cuban population evolved from the eastern flyway population of greater sandhill cranes (Jones et al. 2005).

According to Curt Meine and George Archibald (1996) the surviving birds are limited to thirteen scattered locations in Cuba. They extend from Pinar de la Rio in the west to the Rio Cauto delta in the east, as well as occurring on the Isle of Youth (Isla de la Juventud) and some smaller offshore islands. The birds are found in pine savannas, grasslands, wetlands, and swamps. The total Cuban population has consisted of 550–650 birds in recent years, and is believed to be increasing as a result of stronger conservation efforts.

Although little is known of the biology of this species, in one study forty-one nests on the Isle of Youth were monitored, of which twenty-eight (68 percent) hatched at least one egg. Over five years of study across several parts of the race's range, seasonally flooded plains and natural savannas were the most preferred environmental attributes (Aguilera, Alvarez, and Rosales 2001).

46

More recent studies on the Isle of Youth resulted in the finding of seventy-three nests and the monitoring of forty-four of these. Overall, 84 percent of the nests with eggs hatched at least one chick, nearly half of the eggs hatched, and 54.5 percent of the monitored nests were successful. Predation, disturbance, and flooding were among the causes of nest failure. Only one case of renesting was found (Aguilera, Alvarez, and Chavez-Ramirez 2005).

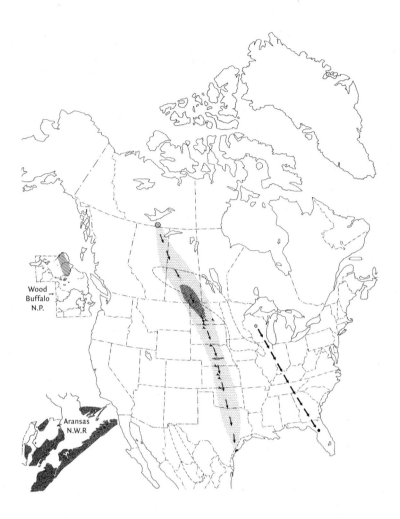

MAP 3. Breeding (diagonal hatching) and wintering (inked) ranges of the whooping crane, together with the migration route (arrows), migratory corridor (stippling), primary staging areas (cross-hatching), and regular stopover points (arrowheads) of the Aransas–Wood Buffalo flock. Broken lines outline probable historic breeding and wintering regions. The general route of the experimental Wisconsin–Florida migratory flock is also indicated by arrows, with the approximate locations of Necedah and Chassahowitzka national wildlife refuges shown by inked and open circles. Adapted and updated from Johnsgard (1991).

Three. The Whooping Crane

Still Surviving Despite the Odds

If any American bird species might be considered the poster child for conservation it would be the whooping crane. No other North American bird has come so perilously close to extinction—its total wild population probably numbered less than twenty individuals in the early 1940s—and yet has managed to struggle back nearly twentyfold, reaching nearly four hundred wild birds in three separate populations by the spring of 2009.

The 1937 establishment of Aransas National Wildlife Refuge, at the center of the whooping crane's wintering area of coastal Texas marked the beginning of a long-term restoration effort by U.S. conservation agencies. But then America was in the midst of both a depression and drought, and it wasn't until after World War II that the plight of the whooping crane began to receive serious attention.

In spite of the protection provided by Aransas, the whooping cranes barely continued to survive. Ignorant hunters killed least thirty-nine adults between 1938 and 1948, holding the population essentially to its pre-Aransas level. A key aspect of the survival of the species was the 1954 discovery of its Canadian nesting grounds within Wood Buffalo National Park, Alberta and adjacent Northwest Territories, when the population was still hovering at only twenty-one adult birds. That development set the stage for major conservation efforts by the Canadian Wildlife Service.

These efforts at Wood Buffalo National Park have included annual breeding ground surveys, searches for nests (starting in 1967 when there were still fewer than twenty breeding pairs), and banding of young. For thirty years (1967–96) there was also a selective removal of eggs (one per nest) from nests, in order to establish captive breeding flocks and begin a new wild flock at Grays Lake. The removal of a single egg from a typical two-egg clutch was not considered a serious loss, since whooping cranes normally succeed in rearing only one chick per year.

A program of color-banding juveniles was undertaken in 1977 (when there were sixty-two adults at Wood Buffalo Park) to document the lives of individual cranes, and continued until 1988. Karine Gil (personal communication) has analyzed the survival and individual reproductive success from these banding efforts. She determined that 20 of the 132 banded birds were still surviving by 2007. All were at least nineteen years old, and one had reached twenty-nine years of age. Annual survival of adult whooping cranes averages more than 90 percent, making them potentially among the longest-lived of American land birds. This degree of longevity is not rare in cranes; several sandhill cranes banded in Nebraska or elsewhere are known to have survived in excess of thirty years. Captive cranes of various species have survived for far longer periods; a Siberian crane (*Grus leucogeranus*) survived to more than seventy-five years at the International Crane Foundation, and a sandhill crane lived to sixty-one years of age at the National Zoo in Washington DC.

As a result of Canadian banding efforts, much information has been obtained on life history and ecology,

9. Adult whooping crane walking

including winter territoriality and pair formation (Steyn 1992), chick survival, sex ratios, and age of initial breeding (Kuyt and Goossen 1987), and the habitats used by migrating subadults (Howe 1985).

Compared with those of lesser sandhill cranes, the migrations of whooping cranes are only about half as long, occur outside the regions of high-arctic storms, and are not subjected to a hazardous Bering Sea crossing. According to data compiled by Ernie Kuyt (1992), whooping cranes of the Aransas–Wood Buffalo flock spend about as much time on their breeding grounds (averaging 164 days) as on their wintering grounds (154 days). In contrast, tundra-breeding lesser sandhill cranes may be on their breeding grounds for only three months, the bare minimum amount of time required to incubate a clutch (thirty days) and rear young to fledging (about sixty days). The spring migration period of whooping cranes averages only seventeen days (versus more than three months in lesser sandhills), and the fall migration thirty days (compared to about four months in lesser sandhills).

On a normal migration day whooping cranes average 7.5 hours of flight time, covering about 245 miles. Flights average 32 miles per hour, but at times may reach 50 miles per hour when wind-assisted. Flights also are assisted by the use of thermals to gain high altitudes, alternated with slowly descending glides that are faster than speeds attained during normal flapping flight. Favorable winds may result in flight durations of nine to ten hours, and distances of 425 to 490 miles.

Collisions with power lines are apparently the most serious threat to migrating whooping cranes, accounting for seven deaths that were documented among migrating birds in the Aransas–Wood Buffalo flock between 1956 and 2006, plus a total of thirty-six known mortalities in other whooping crane populations. Various studies have shown overhead lines to pose a serious survival problem for sandhill and other cranes as well (Stehn and Wassenich 2008).

Since 1983 there has been a significant increase in the numbers of whooping crane juveniles and sub-adults, and a corresponding increase in the breeding population. By 1993 several pairs were breeding south of the original nesting zone, in the Alberta portion of Wood Buffalo National Park. By 2005 three pairs were breeding outside the limits of the park, complicating the need for protecting breeding habitats.

A study by Brian Johns and others (2005) reported that, of 136 banded juveniles, 103 returned to Wood Buffalo Park the following spring, and at least 76 percent of first-time breeders nested within twelve miles (twenty kilometers) of their natal sites. Similarly, Kathy Maguire (2008) found that 82 percent of the juvenile whooping cranes that were trained to migrate to Florida by following an ultralight aircraft during Operation Migration independently returned the following spring to within 4.4 miles (7.2 kilometers) of their initial release site. Such site fidelity is probably related to learning migration routes from parents or near relatives, and is common in migratory species exhibiting long lives and monogamous pair bonds.

The duration and ecology of the portion of the spring migration of whooping cranes from Aransas National Wildlife Refuge to the North Dakota–Saskatchewan border have been analyzed in detail by Jane Austin and Amy Richert (2001). This U.S. segment represents a

10. Adult whooping crane preening

distance of about nine hundred miles, or nearly 40 percent of the total distance to Wood Buffalo National Park.

Among 528 spring observations obtained between 1943 and 1999, the largest number (69.1 percent) were from Nebraska, proving the critical importance of the Platte and other Nebraska rivers to migrating whooping cranes, in spite of repeated political efforts on the part of powerful agricultural interests to downplay its significance, such as efforts to remove the Platte from the areas federally recognized as representing critical habitat for the species. Progressively fewer sightings occurred in North Dakota, Kansas, South Dakota, Montana, Oklahoma, and Texas. Among 486 fall migration records, the largest number (33.1 percent) were also from Nebraska, followed by Kansas, North Dakota, Oklahoma, South Dakota, Montana, and Texas.

Marshy wetland habitats accounted for more than three-fourths of all migrating crane observations except in Nebraska, where marsh records accounted for 56 percent of the total and there were a larger number of riverine observations. During migration the cranes were found to favor wetlands averaging only 7.1 inches deep for feeding or roosting, and having a maximum average depths of 20 inches. The majority of foraging observations occurred on upland sites, typically croplands. During spring these usually consisted of row-crop stubble, with a more limited use of small-grain stubble and green crops. During fall, foraging most often was seen in green crops (such as alfalfa) and standing small grain, with a lesser use of row-crop stubble.

In Nebraska, where riverine records represented 39.6 percent of all sightings, these mostly occurred along the

Platte River, but also included the Niobrara, Middle Loup, and North Loup rivers. Most locations where cranes were observed were more than a half-mile from human developments. Most were more than seventeen hundred feet from the nearest power or phone lines, and average river width at sites used for both roosting and feeding was more than seven hundred feet. About half of all the roost sites and two-thirds of the foraging sites had unobstructed visibility for more than a quarter-mile.

Jane Austin and Amy Richert reported that spring migrations out of the Aransas wintering area typically began in mid- to late March, but were quite variable, and in some years had not begun until early April. By mid-May all the birds had usually reached the Canadian border, although stragglers were sometimes present south of Canada into June. Based on the median dates of occurrences, the peak date for spring migration sightings was April 6 in Oklahoma, April 12 in Kansas and Nebraska, April 19 in South and North Dakota, and April 26 in Montana. The main duration of spring presence in each state ranged from as few as six days in Texas to thirteen days in South Dakota.

In recent years a few single whooping cranes, typically immatures of the previous year, have migrated north with sandhill cranes, often arriving in the Platte Valley in early March, and remaining until the sandhills leave. These are birds that evidently were separated from their parents during the fall migration or later, and associated with sandhills over the winter. By being temporally separated from the later main whooping crane migration they may be lost to the effective whooping crane gene pool, or they may return a season or two later to Aransas.

11. Adult whooping crane uttering unison call

Sites in the Great Plains that have been identified as critical habitat for whooping cranes include Salt Plains National Wildlife Refuge, Oklahoma; Cheyenne Bottoms State Wildlife Area and Quivira National Wildlife Refuge, Kansas; and the central Platte River valley. Other 58 important stopover sites include Nebraska's Rainwater Basin, and Lostwood National Wildlife Refuge and Divide County, both in northwestern North Dakota. Of all these locations, Quivira National Wildlife Refuge had the highest incidence of long-term spring use relative to the Platte, while Cheyenne Bottoms had the highest frequency of fall use. Whooping cranes also typically have a fall stopover period of about two weeks in south-central Saskatchewan. There they feed in grain fields and roost in nearby wetlands at sites such as Last Mountain Lake (used during sixteen of twenty years), Blaine Lake (used during fifteen of twenty years), and Muskiki Lake (used during seven of ten years) (Johns 2005).

The statistical peak of migration during fall, based on median dates of sightings tallied by Jane Austin and Amy Richert (2001), were October 18 in North Dakota, October 22 in South Dakota, October 27 in Nebraska and Kansas, October 28 in Oklahoma, and November 1 in Texas. The usual duration of fall occurrence in each state ranged from as few as ten days in Nebraska to twenty-two days in North Dakota. The fall migration southward thus is on average more protracted than the spring migration, perhaps in part because many adults are then escorting recently fledged young, and there is no great rush to reach and claim preferred breeding territories.

The Grays Lake Egg-transplant Experiment

The experimental cross-fostered flock of whooping cranes that began in 1975 by placing whooping crane eggs from Wood Buffalo Park under the care of sandhill cranes at Grays Lake National Wildlife Refuge, Idaho, has now died out.

Of 289 whooping crane eggs transferred to Grays Lake and placed under greater sandhill crane foster parents, 209 eggs hatched, and fewer than 90 chicks were fledged (about 40 percent), mostly owing to coyote predation and bad weather during the breeding season. Similarly, between 1995 and 2005, 374 nests at Wood Buffalo National Park fledged 149 young (39.8 percent) (Folk et al. 2008). Eighty-five of the cross-fostered cranes made it safely to the wintering area at Bosque del Apache Refuge, New Mexico, and some of them also successfully returned to Idaho.

Sadly, as a result of cross-fostering the birds evidently failed to learn to identify themselves as whooping cranes, and none ever attempted to mate with its own kind, although one hybrid was produced. High mortality rates resulting from power-line or fence collisions and avian tuberculosis also killed many adults, and eventually helped doom the project.

After the mid-1980s the flock underwent a steady decline, and a decision was made in 1989 to terminate the egg-transfer program. The last wild survivor disappeared during the spring of 2002, although one male from the Grays Lake population still survives at Wisconsin's International Crane Foundation, paired with a female sandhill that had been raised by captive whoopers.

The Florida Reintroduction Experiment

By 1989, the decision to abandon additional egg trans-
fers at Idaho's Grays Lake was replaced with a plan to
try to establish a non-migratory whooping crane flock
in central Florida. Whooping cranes had historically
existed there as winter migrants, perhaps until as late as
the 1930s. The site chosen was the Kissimmee Prairie in
central Florida, an area of about eight hundred square
miles where Florida sandhill cranes were already thriving. After obtaining approval from state, federal, and
provincial agencies, the first group of captive-reared
cranes was released early in 1993. The young cranes
had been hatched and reared in facilities of the U.S.
Fish and Wildlife Service's Patuxent Wildlife Research
Center, Maryland, and the International Crane Foundation, Wisconsin.

A total of fourteen juveniles were released in 1993,
followed by nineteen in 1994, nineteen more in 1995,
and additional birds in later years until a total of more
than three hundred had been released. Initially the
young birds were placed in well-fenced enclosures that
proved not to be predator-proof. During the first two
years, two-thirds of the released birds were killed by bobcats. Later, by using enclosures located well away from
known bobcat habitats, survival was greatly improved,
with first-year survival later ranging from about 50 to
70 percent. Over the birds' second and third years of
life there was an 83 percent annual survival.

By 1996 some of the released birds had been seen
forming pair bonds, mating, and even building nests,
raising hopes for the project's eventual success. During
the spring of 2000 three pairs attempted to nest, and

60

12. Adult whooping crane incubating

one of the four-year-old pairs hatched two chicks successfully, the first wild whooping cranes to be hatched
south of Canada in more than a century. In 2002 a pair
of four-year-olds hatched and successfully fledged one
youngster, its sibling having been snatched from the
nest by a bald eagle shortly after hatching. The surviving
chick, named Lucky by the people who had witnessed
the eagle attack, lived long enough to see its parents
nest again the following year.

During 2003 a total of eight nests were built and
three chicks were fledged. By that spring there were
106 birds living in the wild, raising hopes that a flock
of 25 breeding pairs might be attained by 2020. By the
spring of 2005 there were twelve nesting pairs present,
producing a total of nine chicks, five of which survived
at least to the following summer.

As of January 2006, over three hundred birds had
been released on the Kissimmee Prairie. At least fifty
birds were then still known to be alive and were being
monitored. Of forty-seven nesting attempts, only four

chicks had survived to independence. Collisions with overhead power lines have resulted in at least eighteen deaths. There had also been some long-distance dispersal, during droughts, to Georgia, Virginia, South Carolina, and Michigan, venturing of birds into urban settings, and establishment of pair bonds with Florida sandhill cranes. Several individuals had attempted to mate with sandhill cranes, and one was known to nest (unsuccessfully) with a sandhill (Folk et al. 2008).

Between the winters of 1992 and 2003 the population of adult-plumaged birds rose progressively to a maximum of eighty-seven birds in 2001 and 2003, but no offspring had survived until winter prior to 2002, when there was one. In 2003 there were two, and in 2004 there were four. However, no offspring survived to the winter of 2005. Since then a combination of prolonged droughts, high mortality among older age-classes, and a relatively low fledging success by chicks led to a decision to delay additional infusion of new birds. At the end of 2007 the Florida flock numbered forty-one birds, with only one chick having been fledged that year. No chicks fledged in 2008 and in August this population consisted of thirty adults. The project was officially ended in 2008, following an evaluation of its costs and overall low success. In 2009 one chick was hatched from four initiated nests, and apparently survived at least to fledging.

The Eastern Migratory Flock and Operation Migration

Beginning in 2000, an intensive effort began to establish a migratory flock of whooping cranes in eastern North America. This ambitious, stranger-than-fiction adventure required the skills and resources of several private and governmental organizations that together formed the Whooping Crane Eastern Partnership. To test the migration route and also performance and coordination during the many complex parts of this effort, a trial migration occurred using sandhill cranes in 2000. Each year since, the partnership has successfully reared, trained, and flown a cohort of whooping cranes along a 1,220-mile route from Necedah National Wildlife Refuge in central Wisconsin to the Gulf Coast of Florida, with Chassahowitzka National Wildlife Refuge chosen as the initial terminus. Necedah National Wildlife Refuge was selected for the chick-rearing and release site because of its wetland bog habitat and remote location, much like the situation in Wood Buffalo National Park. It is also situated near the crane-rearing facilities of the International Crane Foundation, the source of many of the eggs that were to be used for the experiment.

This imaginative project depended on the skill of aviculturists in rearing cranes that would not imprint on their human caretakers, by using crane-like costumes while rearing the chicks to fledging. Imprinting in cranes actually begins before hatching, so during the last twenty-four hours prior to hatching, the eggs are exposed to the sound of an ultralight engine and the voices of the pilot's imitations of parental crane calls. Fledgling birds are taught to follow the wingless body of the ultralight that is driven by crane-costumed parent figure.

Success has relied strongly on the ability of highly skilled ultralight pilots training the newly fledged birds to follow the aircraft all the way to Florida wintering grounds. Accomplishing that, the hope was that the birds would survive their first winter and independently migrate back to Necedah the following spring, using their memories of the fall migration as a navigation guide.

64   This motorized migration experiment was the brainchild of two Canadians, Bill Lishman and Joe Duff, who formed a nonprofit organization (Operation Migration) in 1993. It was clearly an audacious idea, and was preceded by several years of experimentation by various people with Canada geese, trumpeter swans, and sandhill cranes, using a truck or an ultralight craft to serve as a "lead bird."

When an ultralight craft is used, it must travel at the cranes' typical flapping-flight air speed of about 30–40 miles per hour, and daily flight distances are limited by the ultralight's fuel capacity to about 350 miles. The pilot also must avoid accidental collisions with obstacles such as power lines, and attacks by aerial predators, and somehow keep all the birds together as a single unit.

The first such migration experiment was done with Canada geese in 1993, and the first motorized sandhill crane migrations were attempted in 1995. Attempts with whooping cranes began in 1997, initially by introducing them into groups of similarly imprinted sandhill cranes. Typically four ultralight aircraft are used, three of them leading chicks, while the fourth recovers any birds that may stray or drop out of the flock. A fixed-wing airplane also flies overhead and may move ahead or remain behind as needed. Ground-support vehicles also follow below.

The birds typically fly at heights of about 350 to 1,000

feet, rarely reaching nearly 4,000 feet, and in good
weather may fly up to a hundred miles or more in a day.
The entire 1,220-mile journey south requires a minimum
of a month or more, and may be delayed for days, or
even weeks, during periods of inclement weather. During
the flight south, stops are made at traditional sandhill
crane migration stopover points, including Hiwassee
National Wildlife Refuge in eastern Tennessee.

The first cohort of eight young whooping cranes
made it safely to Chassahowitzka in fifty days, including
twenty-two days while the birds were grounded as a result
of bad weather. During that winter two were killed by
bobcats but in April of 2002 the remaining cranes left
Florida and began their long flight back to Wisconsin.
They independently made their way back to Necedah,
four of them arriving in less than ten days.

In the fall of 2002 seventeen more young whoopers
were led to Florida, and during the following April all
twenty-one surviving whoopers that had wintered in
Florida successfully returned to Necedah.

In following years the number of young birds at-
tempting the flight gradually increased. In 2003 sixteen
cranes made the trip successfully, joining the nineteen
already there. In 2004 fourteen more juveniles made
their way to Florida, and a cohort of twenty juveniles
began the trip in 2005.

This reintroduction effort has included intensive
monitoring by the U.S. Fish and Wildlife Service and
the International Crane Foundation. Detailed histo-
ries have been collected of the movements and social
behavior of each bird throughout the project. From all
these efforts several lessons have become clear. One is
that cranes return in spring to the general area where

they fledged, not the place where they were hatched and reared for a time. The birds, after experiencing a single ultralight-led migration during their first autumn, are capable of retracing the migration route back to central Wisconsin. The birds do not follow the precise flight path that they experienced the previous fall, but rather follow the same general corridor northward—thus, they evidently do not need to rely on specific visual landmarks to find their way.

Weather events while the cranes are migrating back north, such as strong west winds that send the birds off course and cause them to end up on the eastern side of Lake Michigan, may mean that not all birds will make it back to the release area. And birds that, for one reason or another, have missed legs of the ultralight migration by being transported in a crate, easily become lost if they travel north on their own the next spring. However, partnership personnel have successfully retrieved some of these lost birds and moved them back to Wisconsin. At this early stage in the reintroduction, when the flock is still fairly small, it has been judged desirable to concentrate the flock in central Wisconsin to encourage pairing.

The ultralight-led birds learn much from the sandhill cranes that live near them throughout the year, for example, becoming increasingly wary of people in their yearling summer, through association with sandhills. Fortunately, the captive-reared whooping cranes have readily formed pair bonds with other whooping cranes, rather than becoming imprinted on humans or sandhill cranes. Ultimate success of the project will depend on growing numbers of birds pairing, nesting, and successfully fledging young.

66

On their initial return to Wisconsin the yearling birds typically wander for a time, especially females. Summering birds have been seen in North Dakota, South Dakota, Minnesota, Iowa, Illinois, and Michigan, often in the company of sandhill cranes. Many of the birds that had returned successfully to Wisconsin have 67 migrated again to the Chassahowitzka wintering site in succeeding autumns. They often move inland to winter in freshwater habitats, unlike the original Great Plains flock that winters in coastal estuarine habitats. Some of the birds have also wintered outside of Florida, with sightings in South Carolina, North Carolina, Tennessee, Georgia, and Alabama.

Predators caused seven documented mortalities between 2001 and 2005, five of which were by bobcats. There have also been two gunshot deaths, and a few losses from various other causes (Urbanek and Fondow 2008). In spite of these losses, the number of adults and subadults in the flock gradually increased between the winters of 2002 and 2006: 5, 20, 32, 42, and 53.

The International Crane Foundation and U.S. Fish and Wildlife Service have also begun adding juvenile whooping cranes to the migratory flock by rearing chicks in isolation, but without giving them ultralight training. These newly fledged birds are then released directly into groups of experienced whooping cranes at Necedah—the Direct Autumn Release program (DAR). It is hoped that these juveniles will learn their migration route by associating with the older and experienced cranes prior to starting their fall migration. Experiments with sandhill cranes comparing the results of these two techniques suggest that both approaches may be effective (Urbanek et al. 2005).

In September of 2005 four DAR juveniles were initially released in Necedah to join the local sandhill cranes and more-experienced whoopers. In November the four flew south to Tennessee's Hiwassee National Wildlife Refuge. Later two of them continued on to central Florida and mingled with wintering sandhill cranes, while the other two remained in Tennessee.

By the spring of 2006 the new eastern migratory flock had grown to sixty-four birds. A total of twenty-two more began the trip south that fall. Then in February of 2007 disaster struck, with seventeen of the eighteen young at Chassahowitzka Refuge killed as a result of a severe storm and tidal surge that swept over their holding pen. Although one of the young escaped the storm, it later was found dead of unrelated causes.

After accepting this painful loss, another cohort of seventeen birds was added to the population in the fall of 2007. All of these birds made it safely to Florida, after a record-breaking migration duration of ninety-three days. Seven of ten juveniles in the DAR program flew south to Hiwassee Wildlife area in Tennessee, where they overwintered. By the end of 2007 there were seventy-six birds in the eastern migratory flock.

To avoid local disasters such as the storm of 2007, it was decided to split migrating cohorts into two groups, one of which would terminate at St. Marks National Wildlife Refuge, and the other at Chassahowitzka. In January of 2009 seven of fourteen young whooping cranes arrived at St. Marks Refuge, with half of the flock later continuing on to Chassahowitzka. By then there were seventy-three migratory whooping cranes in the flock.

Restoration efforts are now focusing on the crucial

spring breeding period in the Necedah area. By the spring of 2005 seven breeding pairs had been established on or near Necedah, and four other potential pairs were present. At least five of these seven pairs nested that year, two of which laid single-egg clutches. Both nests were unsuccessful (Urbanek and Fondow 2008).

In 2006 five pairs built nests, but predators destroyed two nests, and the other three nests also failed. However, one pair renested, and on June 23 two whooping crane chicks were hatched at Necedah National Wildlife Refuge, the first successful nesting in the historic U.S. breeding range in more than a century. One of the chicks died before migrating, but by the spring of 2009 the other had established a pair bond, and had even laid an egg when only three years old.

Since 2006 the number of breeding pairs in and around Necedah has slowly increased, but no chicks hatched in 2007 or 2008. As of May 2009, the eastern migratory population of whooping cranes numbered ninety-one birds, including twenty-four adult pairs, seventeen subadult pairs, and nineteen unpaired birds.

In the spring of 2009 twelve whooping crane pairs built nests at Necedah, but all had failed by late April. The reasons for this high failure rate are unknown, but perhaps were related to a huge hatch of black flies occurring late in the incubation period, which cause great stress and blood losses to newly hatched chicks. However, four of the pairs renested, and in mid-June a chick hatched from the same parents (the "First Family") that had hatched two chicks in 2006. This chick died of unknown causes near the end of June. However, a second pair nesting north of Necedah, whose eggs had been found to be infertile, hatched a chick from an egg provided by the International Crane Foundation. This chick was still alive as of July 2009.

Of all the crane restoration efforts, this has seemed the most implausible, and yet it is the one that has shown the best signs of success. These include an efficient and mostly correct learning of migration routes on the basis of a single training flight by juveniles, and the pairing and nesting of birds raised by people dressed as cranes. Although all thirty-four initial nestings have failed, three of seven renests have hatched eggs successfully, and one chick has successfully migrated, paired, and laid eggs as a three-year-old.

At Necedah, seven chicks hatched and two were still surviving in late summer of 2010. Eleven additional chicks from the International Crane Foundation would soon join the migratory flock, which then numbered more than one hundred birds.

This program also is perhaps the most touching example of persistent human efforts on the part of a small army of professionals and amateurs to try to save the magnificent whooping crane from extinction. The sight of a group of whooping cranes falling into perfect echelon formation behind a tiny and fragile ultralight aircraft is a vision that tugs at the heartstrings in a way that few if any other human-based bird images can. It must be an unforgettable thrill and honor to be the pilot of such a craft, with the very lives and futures of some of the rarest birds in the world at stake, and having them following obediently behind.

Four. Our Cranes and Their Fragile Futures

Present and Future Sandhill Crane Populations

The most common crane in the world at present is the lesser sandhill crane. As described earlier, this race has two population components. One consists of the relatively small number (probably 5–10 percent) that breed in southwestern Alaska and winter in the Central Valley of California. The remaining 90 percent or more comprise the mid-continent population that breeds on arctic tundra across two continents from northeastern Siberia eastward to western and northern Alaska and across most of northern Canada. This population winters thousands of miles to the south, in widely scattered wetlands from southeastern Arizona east through New Mexico to Texas, and south into the Chihuahuan Desert and altiplano of northern Mexico.

Only during the spring flight north, when during late March nearly the entire mid-continent sandhill population funnels into Nebraska's Platte Valley, can this population be readily counted. The average maximum Fish and Wildlife Service counts for 2002–4 was 375,875 birds, as compared with earlier maximum counts of 510,000 in 1982 and 515,000 in 1985. Between 1982 and 1993 the highest counts occurred between 1987 and 1990, with three-year averages as high as 434,000 birds (Tacha, Nesbitt, and Vohs 1994). These authors judged that survey procedures are probably inadequate for discerning significant population changes from these data. The maximum 2009 Platte count was of 400,000 birds, or slightly more than those of the previous few years. An alternate counting technique, using high-altitude videography, generated higher maximum estimates of 486,000–552,000 birds for the years 2000–2002 (Kinzel, Nelson, and Parker 2005).

Since the 1990s more than a million snow geese have moved from their traditional spring route along the Missouri valley west into this fertile valley, supplementing the million or more Canada geese, cackling geese, and white-fronted geese that have traditionally used the region as a spring staging area. These geese now consume much of the waste corn that has been the crane's primary spring fuel ever since the advent of the region's corn-growing culture that developed after World War II (Krapu, Brandt, and Cox 2005).

This combination of increased competition between the cranes and the geese, and ever-increasing efficiency in corn-harvesting technology, have reduced the supply of available grain for the cranes, and exacerbated the cranes' problems of depositing body fat during their stopover period. During the past twenty-five years the average fat-storage index in Platte Valley greater sandhill cranes has decreased by about half, suggesting that the birds are increasingly arriving on breeding grounds in less than ideal physical condition. Center-pivot irrigation in the Platte Valley has produced far more corn than did previous dry-land agriculture, resulting in the present-day near-monoculture of corn. However, harvesting technology has also progressively improved in recent years, gradually reducing the amount of corn that remains unharvested in the fields (Johnsgard 2008). The progressive dewatering of the Platte has had disastrous

72

13. Three whooping cranes in flight

effects on the ecology of the both the river and its associated sub-irrigated wet meadows. For arctic-bound cranes,
the combination of finding fewer wet meadows (their
primary source of invertebrate foods) and diminished
supplies of corn, their primary carbohydrate food base,
means that there will be decreased chances of surviving
the spring migration and successfully completing the
next breeding season.

Corn-based agriculture mushroomed with the gradual
development of center-pivot irrigation in the mid-1950s,
with a combination of irrigation and fertilizers multiply-
ing the harvests of grain severalfold. Over the following
decades, ever-increasing amounts of water were released
from Nebraska's Kingsley Dam in the North Platte Valley
(the largest dam and impoundment in the entire Platte
watershed) and were diverted directly from the Platte or
were pumped from its closely associated water table for
irrigation. As a result, groundwater levels declined an

average of nearly six feet in the Central Platte Natural Resources District between 1999 and 2006. Not only did groundwater levels decline seriously at this time, but also, after an extended drought and increased upstream surface-water diversions, the Platte River proved to be exhaustible. During that period Kingsley Dam's impoundment, Lake McConaughy, also sank to historic low levels of less than 30 percent maximum capacity. For several weeks during the summers of 2002 through 2006 the Platte completely dried up from Grand Island to Columbus, a situation that had not previously occurred since the drought years of the 1930s.

The nearly decade-long Nebraska drought of 1999–2008 was part of a fairly regular Great Plains phenomenon; since the nineteenth century historic central Great Plains droughts have typically lasted about a decade. In the southern Plains these periodic droughts are often even more extreme, and in 2009 Texas was still being subjected to one of its worst droughts in history. Similar extended drought conditions have also occurred in Oklahoma. The drought-caused loss of wetlands that are important winter habitats for cranes and other water-dependent birds have had devastating effects on the populations of some of these species.

As a part of a related and long-negotiated federal relicensing agreement of Kingsley Dam, its operators agreed in 1998 to set aside 10 percent of the lake's storable inflows as "the Environmental Account." This water would be released for maintaining wetland habitats of the central Platte Valley when needed. Political pressures by powerful agribusiness interests attempted to remove the Platte Valley from its status as critical habitat for four threatened and endangered species (the whooping crane, interior least tern, piping plover, and pallid sturgeon). However, a review by a committee named by the National Academy of Science confirmed the importance of the river to these species (Committee on Endangered and Threatened Species in the Platte River Basin 2005). Additionally, a thirteen-year Platte River recovery plan was initially formulated in 1997 as the "Cooperative Agreement for Platte River Research and Other Efforts Relating to Endangered Species Habitats along the Central Platte River, Nebraska." The Department of Interior and organizations representing stakeholders of the three affected states finally formalized the plan in 2006, after nearly a decade of negotiations.

This plan (the Platte River Recovery Implementation Program) would fulfill the basic requirements of the Endangered Species Act in protecting wetland habitats of the species for which the Platte has been identified as critical habitat. The program's primary function would add and restore nearly thirty thousand acres of wetland habitats in the central Platte Valley, to help protect these four threatened or endangered wildlife species. It would also reduce water shortages to provide flows of 130,000–150,000 acre-feet annually for habitat management by the U.S. Fish and Wildlife Service.

It remains to be seen whether the costly ($317 million) recovery plan will be fully funded and carried out by the participating parties. If Nebraska, Wyoming, or Colorado fails to fulfill its promises, the program might end and the future of the Platte Valley as a primary spring staging area for migrating cranes and waterfowl will be put at great risk.

Increased stress in finding spring food is not the only

danger the cranes now face. "Recreational" crane hunting has become increasingly more popular on the Great Plains since it was initiated in Texas and New Mexico during the early 1960s in response to complaints about crop depredation in rice fields.

76   Legalized crane hunting in the Great Plains states now occurs in Montana, North Dakota, South Dakota, Wyoming, Colorado, Kansas, Oklahoma, New Mexico, and Texas. The popularity of crane hunting has gradually increased in these states, with Nebraska remaining the only central flyway state still lacking an open season. For the thirty-year period 1975–2004, the collective kill for these states, including those birds killed but not retrieved, averaged 15,719 birds per year. There has been a gradual increase in kills over this time frame. For example, between 1975 and 1984 the average total kill annually was 12,010, while between 1995 and 2004 the ten-year annual average was 19,044 birds, an increase of 58 percent (Safina 1993; Sharp and Vogel 1992; Sharp, Dubovsky, and Kruse 2003). During the entire three-decade period between 1974 and 2004 the central flyway crane kill in the United States increased at an average rate of 2.1 percent per year, while the crane population had been increasing at a rate of 0.7 percent per year (Dubovsky and Araya 2008).

Studies of the 1997–2001 seasons in the Plains states indicated that 84 percent of the kill occurred in Texas, North Dakota, and Kansas (Araya and Dubovsky 2008). The total U.S. central flyway kill for the 2005–6 season was 20,063. During the 2004–5 and 2005–6 seasons, Texas hunters accounted for 64.5 percent of the total kill, and North Dakota another 23.4 percent (Martin 2006).

14. Adult greater sandhill cranes fighting

Sandhill hunting also goes on in Alaska, Canada, and Mexico. No recent data are available from Mexico, but the 1995–2001 average seven-year retrieved kill for Alaska was less than one thousand birds, and that of Canada (Manitoba and Saskatchewan) averaged less than five thousand birds over the same period. However, the average three-year 2000–2 Canadian kill was 8,728 birds, suggesting an increasing kill trend similar to that of the United States. Between the early 1980s and early years of the twenty-first century the Canadian kill increased from about 24 percent to 36 percent of the total U.S. and Canadian kill.

Adding the known Canadian and Alaskan kill figures to those for the central flyway states, it is likely that at least thirty thousand sandhill cranes were being legally shot in Alaska, Canada, and the central flyway states in the early 2twenty-first century. Pressures from Canadian hunters have increased to add Alberta to the two other

Canadian provinces where sandhill crane hunting is already legal, in spite of any potential dangers to migrating whooping cranes.

Most recent Platte Valley counts suggest that the mid-continent sandhill crane population now numbers about 450,000–500,000 birds in spring, and since 1998 the central Platte Valley counts (between Chapman and Overton) have peaked at about 300,000 birds, with no clear upward or downward trend evident (Gil and Chavez Ramirez, unpublished manuscript). It has also been estimated (Drewien et al. 1995) that there is a 4.8–11.3 percent recruitment rate for mid-continent lessers and Canadians. Accepting a mean recruitment rate of 8 percent, about 36,000–40,000 young cranes should enter the population each fall. Further assuming a 30,000-bird mortality rate caused by hunters, 75–83 percent of the potential annual population increase is being eliminated by hunters, exclusive of additional fundamental mortality factors such as predation, disease, and accidents. Since protected crane populations have annual post-fledging survival rates of about 85–95 percent (Johnson and Kendall 1997), one would expect an additional loss of perhaps 25,000 birds from non-hunting sources every year.

One must ask why the U.S. and Canadian wildlife services value "recreational" killing of sandhill cranes above treasuring them for their fundamental aesthetic values, as is the case over virtually all the rest of the civilized world. Presumably it allows for the selling of more hunting licenses and migratory hunting stamps, as it certainly does nothing to enhance the public's appreciation of cranes as objects of special wonder and delight. There are now plans to open the eastern populations of greater sandhill cranes (Atlantic and Mississippi flyway) to hunting too; perhaps some administrator in the U.S Fish and Wildlife Service is already dreaming of the day when we can start shooting whooping cranes as special trophy birds as well.

Adding to all these problems is the specter of glob- al warming, and the progressively longer and hotter droughts that have been visited upon the Great Plains in recent decades. Our cranes have preferences for roosting and foraging in water that is rather shallow, roughly six inches deep (sandhills) to no more than about twenty inches (whooping cranes). These shallow wetlands are especially prone to drying up during droughts. Many of the historic playa wetlands of the Great Plains and adjacent Mexico have already disappeared, as a result of evaporation, purposeful drainage, or associated lowered water tables. Canaries might offer a useful warning of dangers for cave dwellers, but our cranes may augur a bleak future for those of us living on the open plains.

Present and Future Whooping Crane Populations

With all the publicity associated with innovative ideas on establishing a new resident Florida flock as well as developing a new Wisconsin–Florida migratory flock, the original Wood Buffalo–Aransas migratory flock of whooping cranes has received relatively little attention. Based on winter counts in Texas, this population increased from 146 birds in 1992 to 257 in 2008. Between 1992 and 1997 there was a net increase of fourteen birds, between 1997 and 2002 a further increase in fourteen birds, and between 2002 and 2007 an increase in sixty-three birds. The 2007 and 2008 seasons added

15. Adult whooping cranes dancing

sixty-one more chicks. Until 2008 this population had thus been increasing at a rate of about 4 percent per year. However, Hurricane Ike and a prolonged drought in Texas brought this hopeful situation to an end during the autumn and winter of 2008–9.

The winter of 2008–9 proved disastrous for the Aransas whooping crane flock. During that season the flock lost 23 of its early-winter 270 birds, the worst year for crane mortality in twenty-six years. From an initial 2008 maximum fall total of 232 adults and 32 juveniles, the Aransas refuge population shrank to a February 2009 estimate by refuge manager Tom Stehn of 253 birds, including 228 adults and 25 juveniles. A later spring count just prior to migration revealed a total of 249 total cranes.

A combination of weather factors was responsible. Texas was then in one of its worst droughts on record, a reflection of La Niña climatic influences, and the flows from the Guadalupe River into San Antonio Bay were the lowest since 1956. As a result, the bay became saltier, and there were fewer blue crabs (*Callinectes sapidus*), which may comprise 90 percent of the cranes' usual winter diet. Wolfberry (*Lycium carolinianum*), which is probably the most important plant food (Westwood and Chavez-Ramirez 2005), also became rare. In spite of efforts to supplement their natural foods with protein-poor corn, close to 10 percent of the flock died over the winter, and probably the surviving spring migrants left Aransas in marginal physical condition.

In spite of these losses, a near-record number of sixty-two pairs of whooping cranes nested in or near Wood Buffalo Park in 2009, suggesting that most of the losses of the previous winter had occurred among young non-breeders. By the end June surveys, fifty-two young had hatched, including ten sets of twins. A total of twenty-two young birds left the park that fall, bringing with them new hopes for the future. However, by early December, only 247 adult birds and 19 juveniles had arrived at Aransas, making the total 2009–10 winter population about 266, the lowest in many years.

In the spring of 2010, a total of 263 cranes left Aransas for their Wood Buffalo breeding grounds. Seventy-four nests were established there, and at least forty-six chicks hatched, including five sets of twins.

For persons old enough to remember when the idea of ever seeing a wild whooping crane seemed little more than a fantasy, the presence of several hundred birds now alive in the wild seems almost too good to be true.

16. Adult whooping cranes in threat postures

We owe the current but still-fragile recovery of the whooping crane to the work of an untold number of dedicated field biologists, aviculturists, and other scientists. We must also thank federal, state, and private conservation groups, and applaud countless individuals, who have helped underwrite the purchase of critical wetland habitats or have funded research needed to produce a viable population of whooping cranes. Very few people are lucky enough to feel as if they have helped save a species from extinction; these are among the select few.

All wonderful and rare things in this world carry a significant price tag, otherwise they would be neither rare nor so highly valued. The opportunity of being able to show our grandchildren sandhill and whooping cranes is a simple choice. We must be willing to protect from destruction their critical riverine and wetland habitats, including both their wintering and breeding grounds, and the beautiful stream that crosses Nebraska like a quicksilver necklace, the Platte River.   83

Beyond its current enormous value to wildlife, the Platte is a historic river along which tens of thousands of immigrants once passed on their way to building a complete America. Wading into the Platte is like wading into history. It is a river that has offered many gifts to us, but that we have almost destroyed in return. Yet gifts such as those provided by rare and beautiful cranes, free-flowing rivers, and biologically rich wetlands are ones that we must be willing to protect, cherish, and finally to pass on to our children as if they were our collective American family's greatest natural treasures—which, in fact, they are.

Appendix

Crane Viewing Sites in the United States and Canada

Note: Many states now have "Watchable Wildlife" or "Birding Trail" programs, and these often include locations favorable for crane watching (see http://www.watchable wildlife.org). Internet searches using a specific state and "sandhill crane" or "whooping crane" as keywords are likely to provide detailed descriptions of sites where cranes have been seen.

Although the following list of more than 125 locations includes many sites where cranes breed, it must be remembered that nesting cranes are extremely intolerant of humans when nesting, and are likely to abandon their nests if disturbed. It is far wiser and more effective to observe wild cranes from blinds or parked vehicles than to try approach them on foot.

Where to See Captive Cranes (All Species)

The International Crane Foundation. This famous non-profit organization (the "World Center for the Study and Preservation of Cranes") is located just north of Baraboo, Wisconsin. It maintains and displays all the species of cranes in the world, including breeding captive whooping cranes, and is the nexus for coordinating crane research around the world. It is also the international center for crane research, and has superb library facilities, with many reference sources available online. It is closed to visitors in the winter. The immediate surrounding area attracts breeding and migrant greater sandhill cranes. Address: E-11376 Shady Lane

Road, P.O. Box 447, Baraboo WI 53912-0447 (608-356-
9462). E-mail: gordon.icf@baraboo.com. URL: http://
www.savingcranes.org.

Zoos and Conservation Centers with Captive Whooping Crane Conservation and Propagation Facilities

Patuxent Wildlife Research Center, Laurel, Maryland. This federal biological research center had sixty-five whooping
cranes in 2008. The center's crane research program
is off-limits to the general public.

Devonian Wildlife Conservation Center (part of the Calgary Zoo),
Calgary, Alberta. The Conservation Center had twenty-
two whooping cranes in 2008. The Calgary Zoo had
two whooping cranes on display that year. Address:
1300 Zoo Road Northeast, Calgary AB T2E7V6 (800-
588-9993).

Freeport-McMoran Species Survival Center. This Audubon
Society facility had eleven whooping cranes in 2008.
Address: 14001 River Road, New Orleans LA 70131
(504-391-7700).

Zoos and Parks

San Antonio Zoo, San Antonio, Texas. Seven whooping cranes
were present in 2008.

New Orleans Zoo, New Orleans, Louisiana. Two whooping
cranes were present in 2008.

Jacksonville Zoo, Jacksonville, Florida. Two whooping cranes
were present in 2008.

Homosassa Springs State Park, Florida. Two whooping cranes
were present in 2008.

Lowery Park Zoo, Tampa, Florida. One whooping crane was present in 2008.

Milwaukee County Zoo, Milwaukee, Wisconsin. One whooping crane was present in 2008.

Where to See Wild Whooping Cranes   87

Florida

Chassahowitzka National Wildlife Refuge. This 30,000-acre Gulf Coast refuge is located sixty-five miles north of St. Petersburg, and is the primary wintering grounds for the experimental Wisconsin–Florida migratory whooping crane flock. Address: 1502 Southeast Kings Bay Drive, Crystal River FL 34429 (352-795-7961). E-mail: chassahowitzka@fws.gov. URL: http://www.fws.gov/chassahowitzka.

Kissimmee Prairie, Florida. In this part of central Florida the experimental reintroduction of whooping cranes has been underway since 1993. It is also an area where there are good chances of seeing resident Florida sandhill cranes, or migratory greater sandhill cranes during winter. One possible route is to take U.S. 441 north out of Kenansville, and search some of the connecting county roads. Or take a dirt road southwest from Kenansville for 6–8 miles into an area of prairies, swamps, and pinelands. Nine miles west of Kenansville on Highway 523 is **Three Lakes Wildlife Management Area** (407-436-1818), a state-owned area of prairie, marshes, and pine woods, where whooping crane releases have occurred. Other areas where whooping cranes have been seen include **Split Oak Forest Mitigation Park** (Orange and Osceola counties) and **Joe Overstreet Landing**, an Osceola County park (407-436-1966) on the east shore of Lake Kissimmee. One may also reach the Kissimmee prairie by driving south from the town of Okeechobee to Lake Okeechobee, or west from Okeechobee to the Kissimmee River.

Texas

88

Aransas National Wildlife Refuge. This 55,000-acre refuge is located at Port Aransas, north of Rockport, and is the wintering grounds for the historic Great Plains flock of whooping cranes, numbering nearly three hundred birds in 2008. The cranes are usually present from mid-November to early April. An "Annual Celebration of Whooping Cranes and Other Birds" is held during February at Port Aransas. Address: P.O. Box 100, Austwell TX 77950 (361-286-3559). URL: http://www .fws.gov/southwest/REFUGES/texas/aransas.

Wisconsin

Necedah National Wildlife Refuge. This 44,000-acre refuge is located three miles west of Necedah (pronounced Na-see'-dah), Wisconsin. Here whooping cranes are raised in captivity and trained to follow ultralight planes south to Florida. In recent years whooping cranes have begun to nest independently in and near the refuge. This is perhaps the best place in the country for seeing whooping cranes under natural conditions, although much of the refuge is seasonally off-limits to reduce disturbance during breeding. Greater sandhill cranes also nest at the refuge, and stage here during spring and fall migrations. An interpretive center is under construction. The nearby town of Necedah sponsors a Whooping Crane Festival each September. Address: W7996 20th Street West, Necedah WI 54646-7531 (608-

565-2551). E-mail: necedah@fws.gov. URL: http://mid
west.fws.gov/necedah.

Where to See Wild Sandhill Cranes

Alaska

Copper River Delta. This south-coastal site, in the Chugach [89]
National Forest, is a major staging area for sandhill
cranes in spring and fall, and also supports breeding
birds. It is also an internationally important staging area,
with up to twenty million shorebirds in May. Address:
Chugach National Forest, 201 East 9th Avenue, Suite
206, Anchorage AK 99501 (907-271-2500).

Creamer's Field Migratory Waterfowl Refuge. This state-owned
preserve on the outskirts of Fairbanks supports a population of several thousand migrating lesser sandhill cranes
returning from western Alaska and Siberian breeding areas
during August and September. The Friends of Creamer's
Field annually sponsor the Tanana Valley Sandhill Crane
Festival during late August. Address: P.O. Box 81065,
1300 College Road, Fairbanks AK 90708 (907-452-5162).
E-mail: creamers@ptialaska.net. URL: http://www.fairnet
.org/agencies/creamers/Welcome.html.

Kenai National Wildlife Refuge, This refuge of nearly two million acres bordering Cook Inlet is an important breeding area for sandhill cranes, which also pass through in
good numbers during migration along the Chickaloon
Flats. Another good viewing area is the Kenai Flats,
near the town of Kenai, where the birds stage during
spring migration. The vicinity of Marathon Road near
the airport attracts cranes all summer. Address: P.O.
Box 2139, Soldotna AK 99669 (907-262-7021). URL:
http://kenai.fws.gov.

Tetlin National Wildlife Refuge. This 700,000-acre refuge lies adjacent to the Alaska Highway and the Tanana River. Up to 200,000 sandhill cranes funnel through the Tanana River valley between April and early June, in what is perhaps Alaska's largest crane concentration. Many remain to breed here, and large flocks also pass through again in the fall. Unlike most of Alaska's major crane-viewing sites, this refuge is partly road-accessible. Address: Mile 1.3 Borealis Avenue, Tok AK 99780 (907-883-5312). URL: http://tetlin.fws.gov.

Togiak National Wildlife Refuge. This wilderness refuge of over four million acres is largely located in the Kuskokwim River delta, which together with the Yukon delta comprises most of Alaska's lesser sandhill crane breeding grounds. Neither is accessible by roads. Address: P.O. Box 270, Dillingham AK 99576 (907-842-1063). URL: http://togiak.fws.gov.

Yukon Delta National Wildlife Refuge. This immense refuge of over twenty million acres is the heart of Alaska's lesser sandhill crane breeding grounds. It is virtually all remote wilderness, and in summer supports more than one hundred million shorebirds and water birds. Address: P.O. Box 346, Bethel AK 99559 (907-543-3151). URL: http://yukondelta.fws.gov.

Yukon Flats and Kanuti National Wildlife Refuges. Yukon Flats NWR consists of nearly nine million acres. It lies along the Arctic Circle in east-central Alaska, between the Brooks Range and the White Mountains, and is a major nesting grounds for lesser sandhill cranes. Like Yukon Delta NWR, it is a wilderness of lowland tundra and wetlands. Kanuti NWR, 1.4 million acres, also straddles the Arctic Circle between the Kanuti and Koyukuk rivers,

90

and also has nesting sandhill cranes. Other wilderness refuges in the Yukon watershed that probably also are major crane-nesting areas are **Koyukuk NWR** (3.5 million acres), **Nowitna NWR** (1.5 million acres), and **Innoko NWR** (3.8 million acres). All three refuges are virtually inaccessible to tourists, and their bird populations are still little-documented. Address: Federal Building and Courthouse, Room 226, 101 12th Avenue, Fairbanks AK 99701 (907-456-0440). URLS: http://yukonflats.fws .gov; http://kanuti.fws.gov.

Arizona

Sulphur Springs Valley. Located about eighty-five miles southeast of Tucson, the state-owned Whitewater Draw (between Bisbee and Elfrida) and Willcox Playa (seven miles south of Willcox) wildlife areas together support about 35,000 sandhill cranes (mostly lessers, with some Rocky Mountain greaters) each winter, mainly from November through February. Both sites are state-owned wildlife management areas and allow some hunting during autumn. A count of 23,386 sandhill cranes was reported during the Audubon Christmas Bird Count of 2007–8 for the Whitewater Draw area (Elfrida count). The cranes are centerpieces for the annual "Wings over Willcox" celebration sponsored by the Willcox Chamber of Commerce in mid-January. Willcox Playa: http:// www.azgfd.gov/outdoor_recreation/wildlife_area_wil cox_playa.shtml; Whitewater Draw: http://www.azgfd .gov/outdoor_recreation/wildlife_area_whitewater .shtml; Wings over Willcox: http://www.wingssover willcox.com.

Arizona/California

Cibola National Wildlife Refuge. Located on the lower Colorado River, with about two-thirds situated on the Arizona side of the river, this 16,000-acre refuge and adjoining areas are an important wintering location for up to about 2,500 greater sandhill cranes from late September to mid-February. Address: Route 2, Box 138, Cibola AZ 85328 (928-857-3253). URL: http://www .fws.gov/southwest/refuges/CibolaNWR.

California

Carrizo Plain Preserve. This 18,000-acre Nature Conservancy preserve has the largest alkaline wetland (Soda Lake) in central or southern California. It is a major wintering area for sandhill cranes, which arrive in October and peak at four to six thousand in January. Address: P.O. Box 15810, San Luis Obispo CA 93401 (805-546-8378). The **Carrizo Plain National Monument**, southwest of California Valley via Soda Lake Road, includes more than 250,000 acres, and is also used extensively by wintering sandhill cranes. For information contact the Guy L. Goodwin Education Center (805-475-2131), which is open from December to May.

Cosumnes River Preserve. This state-owned preserve of 1,100 acres in California's Central Valley near Lodi, Sacramento County, supports about four thousand lesser sandhill cranes from September to late March or early April. The Lodi Chamber of Commerce annually hosts the "Lodi Sandhill Crane Festival" during the first weekend of November. Address: 6500 Desmond Road, Galt CA 95632 (916-6845-2816). For festival information, contact the Lodi Sandhill Crane Association, P.O. Box

1616, Lodi CA 95241 (800-581-6150), URL: http://
www.cranefestival.com.

Lower Klamath and Tule Lake National Wildlife Refuges. These
are two of six refuges in northern California and southern Oregon that comprise the Klamath Basin refuge
system and total over 151,000 acres. Sandhill cranes
breed here, and are common during spring and fall
migration. Address: c/o Tule Lake National Wildlife
Refuge, Route 1, Box 74, Tulelake CA 96134 (916-
677-2231). URLs: http://klamathbasinrefuges.fws.gov/
lowerklamath/lowerklamath.html; http://klamathba
sinrefuges.fws.gov/tulelake/tulelake.html.

Modoc National Wildlife Refuge. This 6,300-acre refuge in
northeastern California supports a population of breeding greater sandhill cranes, as well as large numbers of
migrating cranes in spring and fall. Address: P.O. Box
1610, Mock CA (916-233-3572). URL: http://www.fws
.gov/modoc.

Pixley National Wildlife Refuge. This 6,400-acre refuge is
located near Delano, in the upper San Joaquin valley.
It attracts up to six thousand sandhill cranes from November through March, and may be the best place for
seeing cranes in the southern Central Valley. It is part
of the Kern refuge complex. Address: Kern National
Wildlife Refuge, P.O. Box 670, Delano CA 93216 (661-
725-2767). URL: http://www.fws.gov/kern/refuges/
pixley.

Sacramento National Wildlife Refuge Complex. Sacramento National Wildlife Refuge is part of a 35,000-acre complex
of five national wildlife refuges. They are: **Sacramento
NWR**, of 10,700 acres (916-934-2801), **Delevan NWR**,

93

of 5,600 acres (530-934-2801), **Colusa NWR**, of 4,000 acres (530-358-2666), **Sutter NWR**, of 2,600 acres (530-934-2801) and the still-unfinished **Sacramento River NWR**, with a proposed area of 18,000 acres (530-934-2801). These refuges in the Sacramento valley host large numbers of sandhill cranes from September to March, as well as about three million ducks and a million geese. Address: Sacramento National Wildlife Refuge, 752 County Road 99W, Willows CA 95988. URL: http://www.fws.gov/sacramentovalleyrefuges.

San Luis, Merced, and Kesterson national wildlife refuges (refuge complex in central San Joaquin valley). All these refuges are in Merced County. San Luis NWR is a 7,400-acre refuge located north of Los Banos, Merced NWR is a 10,000-acre refuge nearby to the east, and Kesterson NWR, of 5,900 acres, is northwest, near Gustine. Sandhill cranes of varied races winter in these refuges from September to mid-March. Peak numbers of about fourteen thousand birds occur in mid-November. Addresses: San Luis National Wildlife Refuge: P.O. Box 2176, 947 North Pacheco Boulevard, Los Banos CA 93635 (209-826-3508); Merced National Wildlife Refuge: 7430 West Sandy Mush Road, Merced CA 953412 (209-722-2572); Kesterson National Wildlife Refuge: P.O. Box 2176, Los Banos CA 93635 (209-826-3508). San Luis NWR URL: http://fws.gov/sanluis.

Woodbridge Ecological Reserve (also known as Isenberg Crane Preserve). This state-owned preserve near Galt in San Joaquin County is a wintering site for sandhill cranes. It is located between Sacramento and Stockton, and is divided into two sections, of which only the south unit is open to the public. Some state-owned wildlife management areas (WMA) where sandhill cranes might also be seen are Ash Creek WMA, near Bieber; Butte Valley WMA, near McDoel; Gray Lodge WMA, near Gridley; and Los Banos WMA, near Los Banos. Public access may be restricted on California's wildlife management areas, so advance contact is strongly advised. For information, phone 209-948-2708, or contact the California Department of Fish and Game, 1416 9th Street, Sacramento CA 95814.

95

Colorado

Alamosa National Wildlife Refuge is an 11,000-acre refuge in the Rio Grande Valley near Alamosa. Migrating sandhill cranes are abundant during March and October, with some roosting occurring in the refuge. Address: P.O. Box 1148, Alamosa CO 81101 (719-589-4021). URL: http://alamosa.fws.gov.

Monte Vista National Wildlife Refuge, near Alamosa, Colorado, is a 14,000-acre refuge in the San Luis Valley, and is on the migration route of the Rocky Mountain population of greater sandhill cranes that winters in New Mexico. The Monte Vista Crane Festival is held annually during March in Monte Vista, Colorado. Up to twenty thousand greater sandhill cranes stop in the San Luis valley during their migrations in October and November, and from late February to early April. Address: 9383 El Rancho Lane, Alamosa CO 80101 (719-589-4021). URL: http://www.fws.gov/Refuges/profiles/index.cfm?id=65511.

Steamboat Lake State Park and Stagecoach State Park Wetland Habitat Preserve. These two montane sites in northwestern Colorado are near the state's main nesting region for

Rocky Mountain greater sandhill cranes, which probably nest south to about the San Miguel River. Steamboat Lake State Park (970-879-3922), of 2,500 acres, is located eight miles north of Clark. Stagecoach State Park Wetland Habitat Preserve (970-736-2436), of only seventy-seven acres, is four miles east of Oak Creek along the Yampa River, and is part of Stagecoach State Park. The Nature Conservancy's Yampa River Preserve of six thousand acres is five miles east of Hayden, and is also a breeding site for sandhill cranes. Morgan Bottoms, on the Yampa River in northwestern Colorado, is an important fall stopover area for migrating Sandhill cranes.

Bonny Lake, Jackson Lake, and Prewitt Reservoir state parks, and Adobe Creek, Purgatoire River, Queens, and Red Lion state wildlife areas. These scattered state-owned reservoirs and wetlands in eastern Colorado often attract large flocks of sandhill canes during March and October. Bonny Lake State Park (970-354-7306) is near Idalia; Jackson Lake State Park (970-645-2551) is near Goodrich; and Prewitt Reservoir State Park (970-842-6300) is near Merino. Adobe Creek State Wildlife Area and Purgatoire River State Wildlife Area (719-336-6600) are both near Las Animas. Queens State Wildlife Area (719-336-6600) is near Eads, and Red Lion State Wildlife Area (970-842-6300) is near Crook. In 2005 cranes nested and a chick was fledged at Latham Reservoir (near LaSalle, Weld County), the first Colorado breeding record east of the Continental Divide. Hunting is permitted in Colorado's state wildlife areas.

Fruitgrowers Reservoir and Harts Basin. This reservoir in Harts Basin of western Colorado attracts up to twenty thousand greater sandhill cranes during spring migration, between early March and mid-April. After leaving wintering sites such as Bosque del Apache National Wildlife Refuge the cranes fly north through Monte Vista National Wildlife Refuge, and then stop briefly at this reservoir near Delta after crossing over North Pass or Cochetopa Pass at ten thousand feet or higher. Each late March the local Black Canyon Audubon Society sponsors the "Eckert Crane Days" to celebrate the return of the cranes.

97

Florida

Paynes Prairie Preserve State Park. This park of 21,000 acres is located ten miles south of Gainesville. It supports thousands of wintering greater sandhill cranes, and about fifty pairs of Florida sandhill cranes are resident. Guided nature tours are offered from November to April. Address: Route 2, Box 41, Micanopy FL 32667 (352-466-4100). URL: http://www.floridastateparks .org/paynesprairie.

Oklawaha River Basin. About ten thousand sandhill cranes winter along the upper part of this state-managed river basin (the Sunnyhill Restoration Area, 386-329-4404), in the vicinity of Weirsdale and Ocala. Cranes nest at **Bull Creek Wildlife Management Area** near Melbourne (351-732-1225), and at **Little-Big Econ Wildlife Management Area** near Oviedo (407-971-3500), both in the same general region. Farther to the south, the **Avon Park Air Force Range** (941-452-4254), located just east of Avon Park, is another good place to look for sandhill cranes.

Myakka River State Park. This 29,000-acre park near Sarasota is Florida's largest state park, and one of the state's many protected nesting areas for sandhill cranes. Address: 13208 State Road 72, Sarasota FL 34241 (941-361-6511).

Three Lakes Wildlife Management Area. This large state-managed area includes lakes Kissimmee, Jackson, and Marion, all part of the Kissimmee Prairie, a major nesting area for Florida sandhill cranes. It can be accessed from Kenansville (nine miles southeast), Holopaw (thirteen miles north), or St. Cloud (twenty-five miles north). See also the Florida account in the whooping crane section above.

Georgia

Okefenokee National Wildlife Refuge. This huge (396,000-acre) refuge is the northernmost breeding area for the Florida sandhill crane, with a population of about five hundred birds. It also attracts large numbers of migrating and wintering greater sandhills from November to March. Address: Route 2, Box 338, Folkston GA 31537 (912-496-3331). URL: http://www.fws.gov/okefenokee.

Idaho

Bear Lake National Wildlife Refuge. This 17,500-acre refuge in southeastern Idaho consists mostly of marshes and grassland. It supports a breeding population of greater sandhill cranes, and the birds are also common during spring and fall migrations. Address: 170 Webster Street, P.O. Box 9, Montpelier ID83254 (208-847-1757). URL: http://www.fws.gov/bearlake.

Camas National Wildlife Refuge. This 10,600-acre refuge located along Camas Creek in southeastern Idaho supports a breeding population of sandhill cranes. It also is a fall staging area for cranes coming out of Montana, and host to large flocks of tundra and trumpeter swans during migration. Address: 2150 East 250 North, Hamer ID 83425 (208-662-5423). URL: http://www.fws.gov/camasnwr.

99

Grays Lake National Wildlife Refuge. This 17,000-acre montane refuge hosts the densest known population of greater sandhill cranes (200–250 pairs), and was the site of a cross-fostering experiment with whooping cranes in the 1970s and 1980s. More than a thousand greater sandhill cranes stage here each fall. Address: 74 Grays Lake Road, Wayan ID (208-237-6615). URL: http://www.fws.gov/grayslake.

Indiana

Jasper-Pulaski Fish and Wildlife Area. Thousands of migrating greater sandhill cranes occur on this state-owned wildlife area from late September through December, with peak numbers (ten to thirty thousand) in mid-November. Smaller numbers occur in spring. Address: 5222 North Fish and Wildlife Lane, Medaryville IN 74957 (219-843-4831).

Kansas

Cheyenne Bottoms Wildlife Management Area. This extensive (18,000-acre) marshland is located six miles northeast of Great Bend. It has been classified as a wetland of international importance, and as critical habitat for migrating whooping cranes. During early spring (mid-March) thousands of sandhill cranes briefly stop here on their way to the Platte River, and many stop again in October. Possibly half of the entire North American shorebird population stages here during spring migration. Address: Route 1, Great Bend ks 67530 (620-665-0231).

Kirwin National Wildlife Refuge. This 10,800-acre refuge in north-central Kansas is located around Kirwin Reservoir in the Solomon River Valley. It attracts good numbers of migrating sandhill cranes during spring and fall, and whooping cranes have also been reported during both seasons. Address: Route 1, Box 103, Kirwin ks 67644 (913-543-6673). url: http://kirwin.fws.gov.

Quivira National Wildlife Refuge. This 21,000-acre refuge twelve miles northeast of Stafford is a traditional stopping point for migrating whooping cranes (March to April and mid-October to mid-November). It also supports vast numbers of sandhill cranes from mid-October to mid-December. In 1997 an estimated maximum 94,000 were present, in 1998 the peak was 56,000 and in 1999 numbers reached about 250,000. About 48,000 were seen on the 2007–8 Audubon Christmas Bird Count. Address: P.O. Box G, Stafford ks 67578 (315-486-2393). url: http://quivira.fws.gov.

Michigan

Bernard Baker Sanctuary. This 900-acre site is Michigan Audubon Society's oldest bird sanctuary. It is located near Bellevue in Calhoun County, and is a nesting area for greater sandhill cranes as well as a major fall staging area. Over 8,500 cranes, or about half of the state's estimated total of 16,700 cranes, were observed here in late October 2007. The sanctuary hosts an annual "Crane Fest" in mid-October of each year. Address: 21145 15

Mile Road, Bellevue MI 49021 (269-763-3090). URL: http://www.bakersanctuary.org.

Phyllis Haehnle Memorial Sanctuary. This Audubon sanctuary of about nine hundred acres is located six miles northeast of Jackson, in Jackson County. The sanctuary is a nesting area for greater sandhills, and supports over 3,800 sandhill cranes from late September to mid-November, making it one of Michigan's largest concentrations. A whooping crane was seen there in 2007 and 2008. Address: 6142 Territorial Road, Pleasant Lake MI 49272 (517-769-6891). URL: http://www .haehnlesanctuary.org.

Seney National Wildlife Refuge. This 95,000-acre refuge of marshes, swamps, and conifer-covered sandy ridges in Michigan's Upper Peninsula is a major breeding area for greater sandhill cranes. They are common on the refuge from spring through fall. Address: 1674 Refuge Entrance Road, Seney MI 49883 (906-586-9851). URL: http://midwest.fws.gov/seney.

Minnesota

Agassiz National Wildlife Refuge. This northwestern Minnesota refuge of 61,000 acres consists of northern prairies, bogs, and scattered woodlands. It supports breeding greater sandhill cranes, and up to a thousand or more are present during fall migration. It is located about twenty miles northeast of Thief River Falls. Address: 2296 290 Street Northeast, Middle River MN 56737 (218-449-3115). URL: http://midwest.fws.gov/agassiz.

Boyd Sartell Wildlife Management Area. This state-owned site of nearly one thousand acres is at the southeastern limits of Minnesota's sandhill crane breeding range.

It is located near Faribault along the headwaters of the Cannon River, and consists of both marsh and lowland hardwood habitats. Hunting is allowed here, limiting birding opportunities during fall. Address: Jackson Avenue, Faribault, MN 55021 (507-441-226).

102   Carlos Avery Wildlife Management Area. This 20,000-acre site near Forest Lake, only thirty miles north of the Twin Cities, is a breeding area for sandhill cranes, bald eagles, and many other wetland-dependent birds. Address: 5483-C West Broadway, Forest Lake MN 55025 (651-296-3450). Not far to the northwest is **Sandhill Crane Natural Area**, just outside East Bethel, which is part of a larger cluster of prairie and wetland properties where sandhill cranes have been known to nest.

Crane Meadows National Wildlife Refuge. This refuge comprises more than two thousand acres, plus the associated Crane Meadows Wildlife Management Area and the adjacent Rice–Skunk Lake Wildlife Management Area. They consist of a combination of wetlands, sedge meadows, and prairie that offer nesting habitats for more than thirty pairs of cranes, and a migration stopover point for several hundred more. The refuge is located east of Little Falls, along the Platte and Skunk rivers. It was established in 1992, and is still under development and enlargement. Address: Rural Route 6, Box 171A, Little Falls MN 56345 (320-632-1575). URL: http://midwest.fws.gov/cranemeadows.

Lac Qui Parle Wildlife Management Area, Pembina Trail State Natural Area, and Roseau River Wildlife Management Area. These areas are all important stopover points for migrating cranes. Lac Qui Parle WMA (320-734-44510) is located between Appleton and Montevideo, Pembina Trail SNA

(218-281-6063) is located between Mentor and Crookston, and Roseau River WMA (no phone) is located north of Badger. Hunting is allowed at Minnesota's wildlife management areas, so fall birding opportunities may be limited.

Sherburne National Wildlife Refuge. This 30,600-acre refuge in the St. Francis River valley of central Minnesota is a mixture of wetlands, prairie, and woodlands. It has a population of breeding greater sandhill cranes, and flocks regularly stop over during spring and fall migration. Address: Route 2, Zimmerman MN 55398 (612-389-3323). URL: http://midwest.fws.gov/sherburne.

Mississippi

Mississippi Sandhill Crane National Wildlife Refuge. This 18,000-acre refuge protects the highly endangered Mississippi race of sandhill cranes. As of 2008 it had a resident population of about 130 birds. Refuge tours are provided in January and February. Address: 7200 Crane Lane, Gautier MS 19553 (228/497-6322). URL: http://www.fws.gov/mississippisandhillcrane.

Montana

Bowdoin National Wildlife Refuge. This 15,500-acre refuge attracts up to ten thousand sandhill cranes from mid-September through October. Address: P.O. Box J, Malta MT 59538 (406-654-2863). URL: http://www.fws.gov/bowdoin.

Charles M. Russell National Wildlife Refuge. This enormous grassland refuge of more than a million acres supports large numbers of sandhill cranes during spring and fall migrations. Address: P.O. Box 110, Lewistown MT 59457 (406-538-8706). URL: http://cmr.fws.gov.

Medicine Lake National Wildlife Refuge. This 31,000-acre grassland and wetland refuge in the grasslands of northeastern Montana supports thousands of sandhill cranes during late October, and sometimes also attracts whooping cranes. Address: HC 51, Box 2, Medicine Lake MT 59247 (406-789-2305). URL: http://medicinelake.fws.gov.

Red Rock Lakes National Wildlife Refuge. See Wyoming entry below.

Nebraska

Lillian Annette Rowe Audubon Sanctuary. This 1,900-acre sanctuary is located along the Platte River in the heart of the sandhill crane's spring staging area, about five miles southwest of Gibbon. The Iain Nicolson Audubon Center is open year-round, and provides sunrise and sunset blind tours from early March until early April. A National Geographic "Crane Cam" seasonally provides live streaming video of crane roosting areas via the Internet. The largest blind accommodates up to forty people, and overlooks a roost attracting as many as twenty thousand cranes in late March. Single- or two-person blinds can also be rented for overnight use by professional photographers willing to endure the cold. An Audubon-sponsored "Rivers and Wildlife Celebration" has been held in Kearney annually for nearly forty years during mid-March. Address: 44450 Elm Island Road, Gibbon NE 68840 (308-468-5282). URL: http://www.rowesanctuary.org.

Nevada

Ruby Lake National Wildlife Refuge. This 337,000-acre semidesert and marsh refuge supports breeding greater sandhill cranes, and attracts migratory flocks during spring. Address: HC 60, Box 860, Ruby Valley KNV 89833 (702-779-2237). URL: http://www.fws.gov/rubylake.

Sheldon National Wildlife Refuge. This enormous (575,000-acre) semi-desert refuge supports breeding greater sandhill cranes, and also attracts migrating cranes in spring and fall. Located in northern Nevada, its administrative office is across the border in Oregon. Address: P.O. Box 111, Lakeview OR 97630 (503-947-3315). URL: http://www.fws.gov/sheldonhartmtn/Sheldon/index.html.

105

New Mexico

Bitter Lake National Wildlife Refuge. This 23,000-acre refuge is one of the major wintering grounds for sandhill cranes in the Great Plains, with as many as 72,000 reported here. More than 14,000 sandhill cranes were reported during the Audubon Christmas Bird Count of 2005–6. Address: 4067 Bitter Lake Road, Roswell NM 88201 (505-622-6755). URL: http://www.fws.gov/southwest/refuges/newmex/bitterlake.

Bosque del Apache National Wildlife Refuge. This 57,000-acre refuge near Socorro, New Mexico, is a major wintering area for greater sandhill cranes, and during the 1980s served as the wintering grounds for whooping cranes that had been foster-reared by sandhill cranes at Grays Lake, Idaho, in a failed restoration effort. The refuge offers some of the country's best opportunities for observing large flocks of wintering greater sandhill cranes (up to twenty thousand) from mid-November to mid-February, as well as very large numbers of snow geese and other waterfowl. More than ten thousand sandhill cranes were reported during the Audubon

Christmas Bird Count of 2007–8. The refuge hosts a Festival of the Cranes celebration during the third week of November. Address: P.O. Box 1246, Socorro NM 87801 (505-836-1828). URL: http://www.fws.gov/southwest/refuges/newmex/bosque.html.

¹⁰⁶ Grulla National Wildlife Refuge. This 3,000-acre refuge near Portalis attracts large numbers of wintering sandhill cranes (*grulla* is a Spanish term for cranes); as many as 85,000 have been counted during December. Managed through Muleshoe National Wildlife Refuge. Address: c/o Muleshoe National Wildlife Refuge, P.O. Box 549, Muleshoe TX 79347 (806-946-3341). URL: http://south west.fws.gov/refuges/newmex/grulla.html.

Las Vegas National Wildlife Refuge. This 8,700-acre refuge near Las Vegas attracts large numbers of migrating and wintering sandhill cranes during wet years. Address: Route 1, Box 399, Las Vegas NM 87701 (505-425-3581). URL: http://southwest.fws.gov/refuges/newmex/las vegas/index.html.

North Dakota

Audubon National Wildlife Refuge. This 15,000-acre refuge is located five miles north of Coleharbor, in west-central North Dakota. It provides an important fall staging area for lesser and Canadian sandhill cranes returning from breeding areas during October. Address: 3275 11th Street Northwest, Coleharbor ND 57531 (701-442-5474). URL: http://audubon.fws.gov.

J. Clark Salyer National Wildlife Refuge. This grassland refuge of nearly 58,000 acres along the Souris River supports very large numbers of migrating sandhill cranes during spring and fall, and there is also a record of greater sandhills breeding on the refuge. Address: P.O. Box 66, Upham ND 58789 (701-768-2548). URL: http://jclarksalyer.fws.gov.

Lake Ilo National Wildlife Refuge. This 4,000-acre refuge in the mixed-grass prairies western North Dakota attracts good numbers of sandhill cranes during spring and fall migration, as well as up to one hundred thousand waterfowl. Address: P.O. Box 127, Dunn Center ND 58626 (701-548-4467). URL: http://lakeilo.fws.gov.

107

Long Lake National Wildlife Refuge. This 22,000-acre grassland and marsh refuge in south-central North Dakota hosts very large numbers of sandhill cranes during fall migration, and smaller but substantial numbers during spring. Address: 12000 353rd Street Southeast, Moffit ND 58560 (701-387-4397). URL: http://longlake.fws.gov.

Lostwood National Wildlife Refuge. This 27,000-acre prairie refuge in northwestern North Dakota often attracts migrating whooping cranes, as well as sandhill cranes during fall migration. Address: Rural Route 2, Box 98, Kenmore ND 58746 (701-848-2722). URL: http://lostwood.fws.gov.

Oklahoma

Salt Plains National Wildlife Refuge. This 34,000-acre wildlife refuge and associated state park supports huge numbers of migrating sandhill cranes during early spring and late fall, with up to one hundred thousand ducks, geese and cranes present simultaneously. About 25,000 sandhill cranes were reported during the Audubon Christmas Bird Count of 2002–3. Address: Route 1, Box 79, Jet OK 73749 (580-626-7194). URL: http://www.fws.gov/southwest/refuges/saltplains/history.html.

Washita National Wildlife Refuge. This 8,200-acre wildlife refuge and associated state park supports large numbers of sandhill cranes during late fall and early winter. Address: Route 1, Box 68, Butler OK 73625 (405-664-2219). URL: http://southwest.fws.gov/refuges/oklahoma/washita/index.htm.

Oregon

Malheur National Wildlife Refuge. This remote semi-desert refuge of 185,000 acres in the Harney Basin is a major breeding area for about two hundred pairs of greater sandhill cranes, and an important staging area for sandhill cranes migrating to and from California. About six thousand sandhills are often present in late March and April, and up to fourteen thousand have been reported, presumably of mixed subspecies. During autumn 2,000–3,000 greater sandhills are present, the numbers peaking in mid-October. Address: P.O. Box 245, Princeton OR 97721 (503-493-2612). URL: http://www.fws.gov/malheur.

Sauvie Island Wildlife Management Area. This 13,000-acre bottomland site in the Columbia River valley is an important stopover point for thousands of sandhill cranes. They are present from September to March, but maximum numbers occur in late October, with a few hundred usually remaining over winter. It is located on the western outskirts of Portland. Address: Oregon Department of Fish and Wildlife, 2501 Southwest First Avenue, Portland OR 97207 (503-872-5268).

South Dakota

Lacreek National Wildlife Refuge. This 16,000-acre refuge is located in south-central South Dakota, at the northernmost limits of the Nebraska Sandhills. It consists of shallow marshes and rolling sand hills. Migrating sandhill cranes pass through during late March and early April, and again in October. There are also spring and fall records of whooping cranes using the refuge. Address: HWC 3, Box 14, Martin SD 57551 (605-685-6508). URL: http://lacreek.fws.gov.

Tennessee

Hiwassee Wildlife Refuge. This 6,000-acre refuge in southern Tennessee has developed into a major fall staging and overwintering area for migrating sandhill cranes, with up to 20,000 reported, and an average of about 12,000 remaining at least through December. Whooping cranes of the eastern migratory flock often stop here too. Address: Route 3, Box 178, Decatur, TN 37322 (931-484-9571).

Texas

Brazoria National Wildlife Refuge is a central Gulf Coastal refuge of about 10,500 acres, and an important wintering area for sandhill cranes from October to late February. The cranes can usually be found foraging on the upper prairies. This refuge is part of the Texas Mid-Coast National Wildlife Refuge Complex and also includes San Bernard and Big Boggy national wildlife refuges. San Bernard NWR is located south of Brazoria, and supports up to two thousand cranes during fall. Big Boggy NWR is open to the public for only limited activities. Address: 1216 North Velasco, P.O. Drawer 1088, Angleton TX 77515 (409-849-7771). URL: http://southwest.fws.gov/refuges/texas/texasmidcoast.

Laguna Atascosa National Wildlife Refuge is a lower Gulf Coastal refuge of about 45,000 acres, and an important wintering area for sandhill cranes from October to February. Address P.O. Box 450, Rio Hondo TX 78583 (512-748-3667). URL: http://southwest.fws.gov/refug es/texas/STRC/laguna/Index_Laguna.html.

Muleshoe National Wildlife Refuge is an alkaline playa lake refuge of nearly six thousand acres in the Texas panhandle. From late September or early October through winter this refuge supports vast numbers of lesser sandhill cranes, peaking between December and mid-February, sometimes reaching 250,000 birds. A relatively high count of 93,000 sandhill cranes was reported during the Audubon Christmas Bird Count of 2007–8. Most cranes have left by late February, but a few may remain until early March. Address: P.O. Box 549, Muleshoe TX 79347 (806-946-3342). URL: http://www.fws.gov/southwest/refuges/texas/muleshoe/index.html.

Utah

Ouray National Wildlife Refuge. This 11,500-acre refuge in northeastern Utah attracts of migrating sandhill cranes in spring and fall. The Uinta Basin provides a corridor and fall staging area for sandhills migrating out of Wyoming, while the Heber River valley near Salt Lake City offers an alternate route for birds coming south out of eastern Idaho. Address: 1680 West Highway 40, Room 1220, Vernal UT 84078 (801-789-0351). URL: http://ouray.fws.gov.

Washington

Columbia National Wildlife Refuge. Thousands of sandhill cranes migrate through the Columbia Basin of central

Washington, many staging during March in and around this 23,000-acre sage-desert refuge. Address: 735 East Main Street, Othello WA 99344-1443 (509-488-2668). The town of Othello hosts the annual Othello Sandhill Crane Festival in March. URLS: http://www.fws.gov/ columbiarefuge; http://www.othellosandhillcrane festival.org.

111

Conboy Lake National Wildlife Refuge. This 5,500-acre refuge on the lower Columbia River hosts large numbers of migrating sandhill cranes during early spring. It is also one of a few places in Washington where sandhill cranes have nested in recent years. Address: Box 5, Glenwood WA 98619 (509-364-3410). URL: http://www.fws.gov/ conboylake.

Ridgefield National Wildlife Refuge. This 4,600-acre refuge on the lower Columbia River attracts large numbers of sandhill cranes during autumn, as well as hosting about two hundred thousand overwintering waterfowl. Fewer cranes stop in spring. The Birdfest and Bluegrass Festival is held at the refuge during the second weekend of October. Address: 301 North Third Street, Ridgefield WA 98642 (206-887-4106). Nearby is the **Shillapoo Wildlife Management Area**, a state-owned area of 2,400 acres that is used by large numbers of migrating cranes, a few of which overwinter. Address: 2108 Grand Boulevard, Vancouver WA 98566 (360-906-6725).

Wisconsin

Crex Meadows Wildlife Area. This state-owned 30,000-acre wildlife area in northern Wisconsin's Burnett County is located just north of Grantsburg. Its sedge meadows, brush prairies, and pine barrens attract up to five thousand greater sandhill cranes during fall migration. Except for a central 2,400-acre refuge portion, the area is open to hunting. Address: P.O. Box 367, Grantsburg WI 54840; (715-463-2899). URL: http://www.crexmeadows.org.

112

Horicon National Wildlife Refuge. This 20,000-acre refuge in southeastern Wisconsin is a Ramsar-designated wetland site of global importance, and is the largest freshwater cattail marsh in the United States. Sandhill cranes breed here, and it is a major stopover site for migrating ducks and geese, especially Canada geese. Address: Route 2, Mayville WI 53050 (414-387-2658).

Sandhill Wildlife Area. This 9,000-acre state-owned location in Wood County is a nesting area for greater sandhill cranes. Up to five thousand sandhill cranes gather here during fall, with peak numbers in October. (Large fall staging flocks also can be seen at White River Marsh, Green Lake County.) Viewing facilities include observation towers. Hunting is allowed on the area. Address: P.O. Box 156, Babcock WI 54413 (715-884-2437). URL: http://www.dnr.state.wi.us/org/land/wildlife/reclands/sandhill.

Wyoming

Greater Yellowstone Ecosystem (Yellowstone and Grand Teton national parks, National Elk Refuge, and Red Rock Lakes National Wildlife Refuge). This vast corner of northwestern Wyoming and adjacent southwestern Montana is a major breeding area for the Rocky Mountain populations of greater sandhill cranes. Territorial pairs are often visible in the wet meadows along Flat Creek in the National Elk Refuge (307-733-9212) near Jackson. In Grand Teton National

Park (307-733-2880) favored habitats include the willow flats near Jackson Lake Dam, the sedge meadows behind Christian Pond, and beaver ponds below Teton Point and along the Buffalo Fork River. In Yellowstone Park (307-344-7381), Lamar and Hayden valleys are highly favored, and other good crane habitats exist at Willow Park, Swan Lake Flats, Blacktail Ponds, Antelope Creek, and near Fishing Bridge. At Red Rock Lakes NWR (406-276-3347; http://redrocks.fws.gov) cranes may often be found in meadows west of Lower Red Rock Lake and south of Upper Red Rock Lake.

113

Canada

ALBERTA

Formerly the sandhill crane was a breeding bird throughout much of Alberta but is no longer present in the grassland region. The lesser is an abundant transient throughout much of the province on its way to its arctic breeding grounds. The greater seems to be recolonizing its original sites in inaccessible areas of the Foothills region, including Police Outpost Provincial Park on the border with Montana. The more abundant Canadian race seems to be expanding southward into parts of its former range. During migration, huge flocks of sandhills can be observed, mainly over the eastern half of the province, between late April and early May, and from mid-August to mid-October. They annually occur near Cold Lake (Gus Yaki, personal communication).

BRITISH COLUMBIA

Exeter Lake and Moose Valley Provincial Park. Sandhill cranes (greaters or Canadians) breed at Exeter Lake, just west of 100 Mile House on Exeter Station Road, in this heavily glaciated region of marshes, shallow lakes, and wet meadows in the Cariboo Plateau. About twenty miles farther west on this road is the 6,000-acre Moose Valley Provincial Park, which is a connected series of lakes and bogs with breeding cranes. **Flat Lake Provincial Park**, a 10,000-acre wilderness park located about twenty miles southwest of 100 Mile House, also supports breeding cranes but has very limited vehicular access. For information contact BC Environment, #400-640 Borland St., Williams Lake BC V2C 4T1 (250-398-4520).

114

The George C. Reifel Migratory Bird Sanctuary. Just outside of Vancouver, this sanctuary has a small resident population. Migrants fly over and often stop in during the autumn months. The sandhill is a rare and localized breeder in the Queen Charlotte Islands, and a very rare migrant over Pacific Rim National Park on Vancouver Island (Gus Yaki, personal communication). Contact: British Columbia Waterfowl Society, 5191 Robertson Road, Delta, BC V4K 3N9. Phone/fax: 604-946-6980.

White Lake region. This wetland area near Okanagan Falls attracts a still-undocumented number of migrating sandhill cranes (greaters or Canadians—or both) in April, probably those moving north from staging areas in central Washington to breeding areas in the Fraser Valley and Cariboo Plateau. Access is via Highway 97 and the Fairview–White Lake Road. For information contact BC Environment, #201-3547 Skaha Lake Road, Penticton, BC V2G 7K2 (250-490-8200).

During spring and autumn migration lesser sandhills are seen on migration through the **Okanagan Valley** on their way to the arctic tundra. Greater sandhills, which formerly bred here, are now only seen en route to and from their breeding grounds in the Cariboo-Chilcotin plateau. Nearly all sandhill cranes in the South Okanagan are noted migrating in the afternoon over the valley's western hillsides, during the last half of April in spring, and mainly during the last week of September in autumn. They have also been observed on the ground at **Osoyoos Lake**, **White Lake**, **Trout Creek Point**, and **Crescent Beach** north of Summerland. In spring they are often observed resting at **Knutsford**, just south of Kamloops (Gus Yaki, personal communication).

MANITOBA

Breeding birds can be observed right next to Highway 12 in the extreme southeast corner of the province, adjacent to the Minnesota border. They also occur east of Winnipeg, south of **Seven Sisters Falls**, along a gravel road south from the junction of highways 44 and 11, and are often present in the hay meadow approximately six kilometers east of Seven Sisters Falls along PR 307. They are also present in the southern part of the **Bog River** marshes, reached from the southern junction of highways 11 and 44, east of Whitemouth. Take the gravel road north across the railroad track, following it as it jogs consecutively east, north, east, north, and finally east again, approximately every 1.5 kilometers. Walk northeast along a trail following a power line across a meadow to the wetland complex, where a dike traverses it. Birds found northwest of Lac du Bonnet in summer appear to be non-breeders (Gus Yaki, personal communication). The northern part of the **Whitemouth River** is accessible along Highway 11. It attracts hundreds of cranes from April to mid-June, and again from August to mid-September. Breeding birds should be seen along the edges of boggy forest, and near Seven Sisters Falls. Farther west, near Ross and Ste. Genevieve, breeding birds can often be found.

Big Grass Marsh. This protected site of about twelve hundred acres is a globally significant Important Bird Area, and is Manitoba's most important staging area for sandhill cranes. Up to 6,500 cranes have been reported here during late august and early September. It is located close to the western shore of Lake Manitoba, just west of Langruth, and cranes be often seen in adjacent agricultural fields. For information contact the Department of Natural Resources, Box 24, 1495 Saint James Street, Winnipeg MB ROE 0W9 (204-045-6784).

Oak Lake and Plum Lake marshes. This large marshland area (of about 15,000 acres) south of Virden in the Prairie Pothole Region of southwestern Manitoba is a migratory stopover area for hundreds of sandhill cranes, and also supports many colonial nesting species of water birds. The area is a candidate for listing as a Manitoba Heritage Marsh. For information contact the Department of Natural Resources, Box 24, 1495 Saint James Street, Winnipeg MB ROE 0W9 (204-045-6784).

Rat River Wildlife Management Area. This 2,500-acre provincially owned area in the Red River valley southeast of St. Malo consists of marsh and aspen forest, and is a breeding site for greater sandhills. A viewing mound is present. The Tall Grass Prairie Preserve, of about five thousand acres, is located to the southeast of St. Malo between Tolstoi and Gardenton. Cranes are present here from spring through early fall, breeding in this relict prairie, and families can often be seen during summer along the mowed walking trails. For information contact

116

Critical Wildlife Habitat Program, Box 24, 200 Saulteaux
Crescent, Winnipeg MB R3J 3W3 (204-945-7775).

The Pas–Saskatchewan River Delta. This Important Bird Area
of subarctic boreal forest extends from the Saskatche-
wan-Manitoba border east to Cedar Lake, and includes
the Saskatchewan (and its delta), and the Carrot and
Pasquia rivers. It is a breeding area for sandhill cranes
and hosts a still-unknown number of migrating cranes
during fall; at least two thousand have been seen along
the Pasquia River. It is a wilderness area, with The Pas
being the only regional town of any size.

117

NORTHWEST TERRITORIES

Sandhill cranes migrate and breed in low numbers
throughout most of the continental mainland and the
southernmost arctic islands. They can be readily found
in the dune ridge area east of Sachs Harbour on **Banks
Island**. They have been observed by canoeists and raf-
ters, during migration in late August at Virginia Falls in
Nahanni National Park. They have also be seen in autumn over the **Liard River** between Nahanni Butte and
Fort Simpson (Gus Yaki, personal communication).

NUNAVUT

Sandhill cranes are observed in summer at Sila Lodge
on **Wager Bay**, near the upper coast of Hudson Bay.

ONTARIO

The sandhill crane now breeds again in fair numbers
in the **Algoma District** and in the Hudson Bay Lowlands, particularly near the shoreline of James Bay, from

Moosonee northward, where it had formerly become extirpated. It also breeds in large muskeg bogs in the western **Rainy River District** near Lake of the Woods in extreme western Ontario, adjacent to Manitoba and Minnesota. In the more southern reaches, it is currently recolonizing territory lost early in the last century due to agricultural development, mainly in the **Sault Ste. Marie**, **Manitoulin Island**, and northern Bruce Peninsula areas. Just east of Ottawa at **Mer Bleue Bog** a small population now breeds, and a small population has become established at **Big Creek Marsh** at Long Point on Lake Erie. Birds have also recently bred in the southern part of the Niagara region (Gus Yaki, personal communication).

Spy Bay, Marsh Lake. This bay in Manitoulin Island is a provincial Important Bird Area, and an important fall staging site for sandhill cranes. The north shore of Lake Huron, near Disbarat, is also used for staging.

Long Point Bird Observatory. This well-known birding area is easily accessible and is used by moderate numbers of sandhill cranes during fall migration.

SASKATCHEWAN

Last Mountain Lake National Wildlife Area. This 38,000-acre site is Canada's prime location for seeing large groups of sandhill cranes; up to fifty thousand may stop here during fall migration in September and October. It is located at the north end of Last Mountain Lake, about fifty miles north and fifteen miles west of Regina. Wetlands cover about a fifth of the 41,000-acre area; the rest is mostly of mixed-grass prairie. Address: P.O. Box 280, Simpson SK SOG 4MO (306-836-3022). **Stalwart**

National Wildlife Area (3,800 acres) is nearby (just east of Stalwart) and is also used by migrating sandhill cranes. **Kutawagan Lake**, a prairie lake twelve miles northeast of Nokomis, is also nearby and is an important gathering place for sandhill cranes. Whooping cranes have sometimes been seen at Last Mountain Lake, as well as at several north-central Saskatchewan lakes, including Buffer (northeast of Saskatoon), Radisson (near Radisson SK), and Midnight (north of Fairholme). For information contact Environment Canada, Twin Atria Building, 2nd Floor, 4999 98th Avenue, Edmonton, AB T6B 2X3.

Quill Lakes International Bird Area. These three lakes (Big Quill, Little Quill, and Foam), the largest saline lakes in Canada, are located near Wadena, and are a recognized wetland site of international importance (Ramsar). This provincial area of more than 100,000 acres seasonally supports up to 45,000 sandhill cranes, as well as about 400,000 ducks, 200,000 shorebirds, and 200,000 geese. The **Wadena Wildlife Wetlands/Quill Lakes Interpretive Area** has several miles of trails, a boardwalk, and observation tower on Little Quill Lake. **Foam Lake Heritage Marsh** is a 4,000-acre wetland with hiking trails and viewing sites on Foam Lake. Visitor centers are located at Foam Lake, Wynyard, and Wadena (306-782-9582). For information contact Environment Canada, Twin Atria Building, 2nd Floor, 4999 98th Avenue, Edmonton AB T6B 2X3.

South Saskatchewan River. Miry Bay and Galloway Bay, about northwest of Swift Current, are at the west end of impounded Diefenbaker Lake. Together with a thirty-mile stretch of the river, they comprise a provincial Important

Bird Area that may hold up to 160,000 sandhill cranes during fall migration. The area south of Lecadena and the vicinity of Cabri are especially attractive, but birds use the river valley from Cabri west for about fifty miles to Leader. The downstream stretch of the South Saskatchewan River between Saskatoon and Outlook is also regularly used by migrating sandhill cranes. For information contact Environment Canada, Twin Atria Building, 2nd Floor, 4999 98th Avenue, Edmonton AB T6B 2X3.

YUKON TERRITORY

Pelly River Valley. Thousands, probably tens of thousands, of sandhill cranes pass through this steep valley (the Tintina Trench, between the Pelly and Selwyn ranges) in southern Yukon on their way to Alaska's Yukon valley in May. The Crane and Sheep Viewing Festival is held annually in mid-May at Faro (the sheep are Fannin's bighorns). For information on the festival contact the Town of Faro (867-994-2728, info@faroyukon.com).

References

General References

Archibald, G. W., and C. D. Meine. 1996. Family Gruidae. In *Handbook of the Birds of the World, Vol. 3. Hoatzins to Auks.*, ed. J. del Hoyo, A. Elliott, and J. Sargatal. 60–89. Barcelona, Spain: Lynx Editions.

Chavez-Ramirez, F., ed. 2005. *Proceedings of the Ninth North American Crane Workshop*, Sacramento, California. Seattle: North American Crane Working Group.

Ellis, D. H., ed. 2001. *Proceedings of the Eighth North American Crane Workshop*, Albuquerque, New Mexico. Seattle: North American Crane Working Group.

Ellis, D. H., G. F. Gee, and C. M. Mirande, ed. 1996. *Cranes: Their Biology, Husbandry and Conservation.* Washington DC: National Biological Service, and Baraboo WI: International Crane Foundation.

Folk, M. J., and S. A. Nesbitt, ed. 2008. *Proceedings of the Tenth North American Crane Workshop*, Zacatecas City, Mexico. Gambier OH: North American Crane Working Group.

Godfrey, W. E. 1986. *The Birds of Canada.* 2nd. ed. Ottawa: National Museum of Natural Sciences.

Harris, J. T. 2008. Cranes respond to climate change. *The Bugle* 34 (3): 1–3, 14–15.

Hughes, J. 2008. *Cranes: A Natural History of a Bird in Crisis.* Tonawanda NY: Firefly Books.

International Union for Conservation of Nature and Natural Resources (IUCN). 1994. IUCN *Red List Categories.* Gland, Switzerland: International Union for the Conservation of Nature and Natural Resources.

Johnsgard, P. A. 1979. *Birds of the Great Plains: Breeding Species and their Distribution.* Lincoln: University of Nebraska Press.

———. 1983. *Cranes of the World*. Bloomington: Indiana University Press.

———. 1991. *Crane Music: A Natural History of American Cranes*. Washington DC: Smithsonian Institution Press.

Lewis, J. C., ed. 1976. *Proceedings of the International Crane Workshop*, Baraboo, Wisconsin. Stillwater: Oklahoma State University.

———. 1979. *Proceedings of the 1978 Crane Workshop*, Rockport, Texas. Fort Collins: Colorado State University Printing Service.

———. 1982. *Proceedings of the 1981 Crane Workshop*, Grand Teton National Park, Wyoming. Tavernier FL: National Audubon Society.

———. 1987. *Proceedings of the 1985 Crane Workshop*, Grand Island, Nebraska. Grand Island NE: Platte River Whooping Crane Maintenance Trust and U.S. Fish and Wildlife Service.

Meine, C. D., and G. W. Archibald, ed. 1996. *The Cranes: Status Survey and Action Plan*. Gland, Switzerland: International Union for Conservation of Nature and Natural Resources.

Stahlecker, D. W., and R. P. Urbanek, ed. 1992. *Proceedings of the Sixth North American Crane Workshop*, Regina, Saskatchewan. Grand Island NE: North American Crane Working Group.

Urbanek, R. P., and D. W. Stahlecker, ed. 1997. *Proceedings of the Seventh North American Crane Workshop*, Biloxi, Mississippi. Grand Island NE: North American Crane Working Group.

Von Treuenfels, C. A. 2006. *The Magic of Cranes*. New York: Harry Abrams.

Walkinshaw, L. H. 1973. *Cranes of the World*. New York: Winchester Press.

Wood, D. A., ed. 1992. *Proceedings of the 1988 North American Crane Workshop*, Lake Wales, Florida; Florida Game and

Fresh Water Fish Commission, Nongame Wildlife Program Technical Report #12. Tallahassee: Florida Game and Fresh Water Fish Commission.

Sandhill Crane

Aikens, R. 2009. The Southwest's triple crown of wintering cranes. *Arizona Wildlife Views* 52 (1): 1216.

Aldrich, J. W. 1979. Status of the Canadian sandhill crane. In *Proceedings of the 1978 Crane Workshop*, Rockport, Texas, ed. J. C. Lewis, 139–48. Fort Collins: Colorado State University Printing Service.

Aguilera, X. G., V. B. Alvarez, and F. Chavez-Ramirez. 2005. Nesting ecology and productivity of the Cuban sandhill crane on the Isle of Youth, Cuba. In *Proceedings of the Ninth North American Crane Workshop*, Sacramento, California, ed. F. Chavez-Ramirez, 225–36. Baraboo WI: North American Crane Working Group.

Aguilera, X. G., V. B. Alvarez, and J. R. Rosales. 2001. Distribution, abundance and reproduction of the Cuban sandhill crane (*Grus canadensis nesiotes*). In *Proceedings of the Eighth North American Crane Workshop*, Albuquerque, New Mexico, ed. D. H. Ellis, 216. Seattle: North American Crane Working Group.

Araya, A. C., and J. A. Dubvosky. 2008. Temporal distribution of harvested mid-continent sandhill crane within the Central Flyway states during the 1997–2001 hunting seasons. In *Proceedings of the Tenth North American Crane Workshop*, Zacatecas City, Mexico, ed. M. J. Folk and S. A. Nesbitt, 50–57. Gambier OH: North American Crane Working Group.

Ball, J., T. E. Austin, and A. Henry. 2003. Populations and nesting ecology of sandhill cranes at Grays Lake, Idaho, 1997–2000. Missoula MT: U.S. Geological Survey, Cooperative Wildlife Research Unit.

Ballard, B. M., and J. E. Thompson. 2000. Winter diets of

sandhill cranes from central and coastal Texas. *Wilson Bulletin* 112:26–38.

Bennett, A., and L. Bennett. 1990. Productivity of sandhill cranes in Okefenokee Swamp, Georgia. *Journal of Field Ornithology* 61:224–31.

Benning, D. S., R. C. Drewien, D. H. Johnson, W. M. Brown, and E. L. Boeker, 1997. Spring population estimates of Rocky Mountain sandhill cranes in Colorado. In *Proceedings of the Seventh North American Crane Workshop*, Biloxi, Mississippi, ed. R. P. Urbanek and D. W. Stahlecker, 165–72. Grand Island NE: North American Crane Working Group.

Boeker, E. L., J. W. Aldrich, and W. S. Huey. 1961. Study of experimental crane hunting season in New Mexico during January, 1961. U.S. Fish and Wildlife Service, *Special Scientific Report (Wildlife)* No. 63.

Breckenridge, W. J. 1945. Nebraska crane flight. *Flicker* 17:79–81.

Central Migratory Shore and Upland Game Bird Technical Committee. 1993. Management guidelines for mid-continent sandhill cranes. Report prepared for the Central Flyway Waterfowl Council. Golden CO: Pacific Flyway Waterfowl Council, U.S. Fish and Wildlife Service.

Chavez-Ramirez, F. 2005. New locations and range extensions of wintering sandhill cranes in central northern Mexico. In *Proceedings of the Ninth North American Crane Workshop*, Sacramento, California, ed. F. Chavez-Ramirez, 173–78. Baraboo WI: North American Crane Working Group.

———. 2008. Temporal dynamic and flock characteristics of sandhill cranes in the Platte Valley, Nebraska. In *Proceedings of the Tenth North American Crane Workshop*, Zacatecas City, Mexico, M. J. Folk and S. A. Nesbitt, 162. Gambier OH: North American Crane Working Group.

Cooper, J. M. 1996. Status of the sandhill crane in British Columbia. *Wildlife Bulletin*, Vol. B–83:1–40.

Drewien, R., W. M. Brown, and D. S. Benning. 1996. Distribution and abundance of sandhill cranes in Mexico. *Journal of Wildlife Management* 60:270–85.

Drewien, R., W. M. Brown, and W. L. Kendall. 1995. Recruitment in Rocky Mountain greater sandhill cranes and comparison with other crane populations. *Journal of Wildlife Management* 59:339–56.

Dubovsky, J. A., and A. C. Araya. 2008. Hunting success for mid-continent sandhill cranes in the Central Flyway: Comparing current and historic results. In *Proceedings of the Tenth North American Crane Workshop*, Zacatecas City, Mexico, ed. M. J. Folk and S. A. Nesbitt, 58–64. Gambier OH: North American Crane Working Group.

Faanes, C., and M. J. LeValley. 1993. Is the distribution of sandhill cranes on the Platte Valley changing? *Great Plains Research* 3:297–304.

Gil, K., and F. Chavez-Ramirez. Temporal-spatial distribution and abundance of roosting sandhill cranes in the Central Platte River Valley, Nebraska USA: 2002–2009. Unpublished manuscript.

Gilligan, J., M. Smith, D. Rogers, and A. Contreras. 1993. *Birds of Oregon: Status and Distribution.* McMinniville OR: Cinclus Publications.

Glenn, T. C., J. E. Thompson, B. M. Ballard, J. A. Roberson, and J. O. French. 2002. Mitochondrial DNA variation among wintering midcontinent Gulf Coast sandhill cranes. *Journal of Wildlife Management* 66:339–48.

Grier, R. 2009. Cranes on the North Platte. *NEBRASKAland* 87(2): 42–45.

Hayes, M. A., J. A. Barzen, and H. B. Britten. 2008. Mate fidelity in a dense breeding population of sandhill cranes In *Proceedings of the Tenth North American Crane Workshop*, Zacatecas City, Mexico, ed. M. J. Folk and S. A. Nesbitt, 168. Gambier OH: North American Crane Working Group.

125

Hayes, M. A., H. B. Britten, and J. A. Barzen. 2008. Extra-pair paternity in sandhill cranes. In *Proceedings of the Tenth North American Crane Workshop*, Zacatecas City, Mexico, ed. M. J. Folk and S. A. Nesbitt, 167. Gambier OH: North American Crane Working Group.

Hereford, S. G., and T. E. Grazia. 2008. Mississippi sandhill crane conservation update, 2003–2005. In *Proceedings of the Tenth North American Crane Workshop*, Zacatecas City, Mexico, ed. M. J. Folk and S. A. Nesbitt, 156. Gambier OH: North American Crane Working Group.

Herter, D. R. 1982. Habitat use and harassment of sandhill cranes staging on the eastern Copper River Delta, Alaska. Master's thesis, University of Alaska, Fairbanks.

Hjertaas, D. G., D. H. Ellis, B. W. Johns, and S. L. Moon. 2001. Tracking sandhill crane migration from Saskatchewan to the Gulf Coast. In *Proceedings of the Eighth North American Crane Workshop*, Albuquerque, New Mexico, ed. D. H. Ellis, 57–61. Seattle: North American Crane Working Group.

Iverson, G. C., P. A. Vohs, and T. C. Tacha. 1985. Distribution and abundance of sandhill cranes wintering in western Texas. *Journal of Wildlife Management* 49:250–55.

Ivey, G. L., and C. P. Herzinger. 2008. Sandhill crane wintering ecology in the Sacramento–San Joaquin Delta, California. In *Proceedings of the Tenth North American Crane Workshop*, Zacatecas City, Mexico, ed. M. J. Folk and S. A. Nesbitt, 164. Gambier OH: North American Crane Working Group.

Ivey, G. L., C. P. Herzinger, and T. J. Hoffmann. 2005. Annual movements of Pacific Coast sandhill cranes. In *Proceedings of the Ninth North American Crane Workshop*, Sacramento, California, ed. F. Chavez-Ramirez, 25–35. Baraboo WI: North American Crane Working Group.

Johnsgard, P. A. 2002. Nebraska's sandhill crane populations, past, present and future. *Nebraska Bird Review* 70:175–77.

http://digitalcommons.unl.edu/biosciornithology/16
(accessed April 21, 2010)

———. 2003. Great gathering on the Great Plains. *National Wildlife* 41 (3): 20–29.

———. 2008. *The Platte: Channels in Time.* 2nd ed. Lincoln: University of Nebraska Press.

Johnson, D. H., J. E. Austin, and J. A. Shaffer. 2005. A fresh look at the taxonomy of midcontinental sandhill cranes. In *Proceedings of the Ninth North American Crane Workshop*, Sacramento, California, ed. F. Chavez-Ramirez, 37–45. Baraboo WI: North American Crane Working Group.

Johnson, D. H., and W. L. Kendall. 1997. Modeling the population of Gulf Coast sandhill cranes. In *Proceedings of the Seventh North American Crane Workshop*, Biloxi, Mississippi, ed. R. P. Urbanek and D. W. Stahlecker, 173–80. Grand Island NE: North American Crane Working Group.

Jones, K. L., F. Chavez-Ramirez, X. G. Aguilera, L. Tortella, and M. V. Ashley. 2005. Genetic assessment of non-migratory sandhill crane populations. In *Proceedings of the Ninth North American Crane Workshop*, Sacramento, California, ed. F. Chavez-Ramirez, 250. Baraboo WI: North American Crane Working Group.

Kendall, W. L., D. H. Johnson, and S. C. Kohn, 1997. Subspecies composition of sandhill crane harvest in North Dakota. In *Proceedings of the Seventh North American Crane Workshop*, Biloxi, Mississippi, ed. R. P. Urbanek and D. W. Stahlecker, 201–8. Grand Island NE: North American Crane Working Group.

Kessel, B. 1984. Migration of sandhill cranes, *Grus canadensis*, in east-central Alaska, with routes through Alaska and western Canada. *Canadian Field-Naturalist* 98:279–92.

Kingery, H. E., ed. 1998. *Colorado Breeding Bird Atlas.* Denver: Colorado Bird Atlas Partnership and Colorado Division of Wildlife.

Kinzel, P. J., J. M. Nelson, and R. S. Parker. 2005. Assessing sandhill crane roosting habitat along the Platte River, Nebraska. *USGS Fact Sheet* 2005:3029.

Krapu, G. L. 2001. Satellite telemetry: A powerful new tool for studying sandhill cranes. *Braided River* 14:1–5.

———. 2005. Satellite telemetry provides a revealing look at the phantom of the plains. *Braided River* 21:6–9.

Krapu, G. L., and D. A. Brandt. 2008. Spring migratory habits and breeding distribution of lesser sandhill cranes that winter in west-central New Mexico and Arizona. In *Proceedings of the Tenth North American Crane Workshop*, Zacatecas City, Mexico, ed. M. J. Folk and S. A. Nesbitt, 43–49. Gambier OH: North American Crane Working Group.

Krapu, G. L., D. A. Brandt, D. A. Buhl, and G. W. Lingle. 2005. Evidence of a decline in fat storage in mid-continent sandhill cranes in Nebraska during spring: A preliminary assessment. In *Proceedings of the Ninth North American Crane Workshop*, Sacramento, California, ed. F. Chavez-Ramirez, 179–84. Baraboo WI: North American Crane Working Group.

Krapu, G. L., D. A. Brandt, and R. R. Cox Jr. 2005. Do arctic-nesting geese compete with sandhill cranes for waste corn in the central Platte Valley, Nebraska? In *Proceedings of the Ninth North American Crane Workshop*, Sacramento, California, ed. F. Chavez-Ramirez, 185–91. Baraboo WI: North American Crane Working Group.

Krapu, G., K. J. Reiecke, D. G. Jorde, and S. G. Simpson. 1995. Spring staging ecology of midcontinent greater white-fronted geese. *Journal of Wildlife Management* 59:736–46.

Kruse, K., D. E. Sharp, and J. A. Dubovsky. 2008. Population status, hunting regulations and harvests of the Rocky Mountain population of greater sandhill cranes, 1981–2005. In *Proceedings of the Tenth North American Crane Workshop*, Zacatecas City, Mexico, ed. M. J. Folk and

S. A. Nesbitt, 71–75. Gambier OH: North American Crane Working Group.

Letourneau, V., and A. Morrier. 1993. Sandhill crane. In *The Breeding Birds of Quebec: Atlas of the Breeding Birds of Southern Quebec*, ed. J. Guthier and Y. Aubry, 113–14. Foy, Quebec: Canadian Wildlife Service.

Lewis, J. C. 1977. Sandhill crane. In *Management of Migratory Shore and Upland Game Birds of North America*, ed. G. C. Sanderson, 5–43. Washington DC: International Association of Fish and Wildlife Agencies.

———. 1979. Taxonomy, food and feeding habitat of sandhill cranes, Platte Valley, Nebraska. In *Proceedings of the 1978 Crane Workshop*, Rockport, Texas, ed. J. C. Lewis, 21–28. Fort Collins: Colorado State University Printing Service.

Littlefield, C. D., and G. L. Ivey. 2002. *Washington State Recovery Plan for the Sandhill Crane.* Olympia: Washington Department of Fish and Wildlife.

Martin, E. M. 2006. *Sandhill Crane Harvest and Hunter Activity in the Central Flyway during the 2005–2006 Hunting Season*, U.S. Fish and Wildlife Service, Division of Migratory Bird Management, http://www.fws.gov/migratorybirds/newreportspublications/hip/hip.htm.

Montgomery, J. B. 2008. Trends in sandhill crane numbers in eastern New Mexico. In *Proceedings of the Tenth North American Crane Workshop*, Zacatecas City, Mexico, ed. M. J. Folk and S. A. Nesbitt, 37–39. Gambier OH: North American Crane Working Group.

Nesbitt, S. 1992. First reproductive success and individual productivity in Florida sandhill cranes. *Journal of Wildlife Management* 56:573–77.

———. 1997. Florida sandhill crane (*Grus canadensis pratensis*), family Gruidae, order Gruiformes. In *Rare and Endangered Biota of Florida, Vol. 5 (Birds)*, ed. J. A. Rogers, H. Kale, and H. Smith, 219–29. Gainesville: University Press of Florida.

Nesbitt, S., M. J. Folk, S. T. Schwikert, and J. A. Schmidt. 2001. Aspects of reproduction and pair bonds in Florida sandhill cranes. In *Proceedings of the Eighth North American Crane Workshop*, Albuquerque, New Mexico, ed. D. Ellis, 31–35. Seattle: North American Crane Working Group.

Nesbitt, S., and J. L. Hatchitt. 2008. Trends in habitat and population of Florida sandhill cranes. In *Proceedings of the Tenth North American Crane Workshop*, Zacatecas City, Mexico, ed. M. J. Folk and S. A. Nesbitt, 40–42. Gambier OH: North American Crane Working Group.

Nesbitt, S., and S. T. Schwikert. 2008. Survival and sources of mortality in Florida sandhill crane chicks–hatching to fledging. In *Proceedings of the Tenth North American Crane Workshop*, Zacatecas City, Mexico, ed. M. J. Folk and S. A. Nesbitt, 86–89. Gambier OH: North American Crane Working Group.

Nesbitt, S. A., and T. C. Tacha. 1997. Monogamy and productivity in sandhill cranes. In *Proceedings of the Seventh North American Crane Workshop*, Biloxi, Mississippi, ed. R. P. Urbanek and D. W. Stahlecker, 10–13. Grand Island NE: North American Crane Working Group.

Nesbitt, S., and K. S. Williams. 1990. Home range and habitat use of Florida sandhill cranes. *Journal of Wildlife Management* 54:92–96.

Peterson, J. L., R. Bischof, G. L. Krapu, and A. L. Szalanski. 2003. Genetic variation in the mid-continent population of sandhill cranes, *Grus canadensis. Biochemical Genetics* 41:1–12.

Petrula, M. J., and T. C. Rothe. 2005. Migration chronology, routes, and distribution of Pacific Flyway population lesser sandhill cranes. *Proceedings of the Ninth North American Crane Workshop*, Sacramento, California, ed. F. Chavez-Ramirez, 53–67. Baraboo WI: North American Crane Working Group.

Pogson T. H., and S. M. Lindstedt. 1991. Distribution and status of large sandhill cranes (*Grus canadensis tabida*), wintering in California's Central Valley. *Condor* 93:266–78.

Renner, L., P. Gray and V. Graham. 1991. *Greater Sandhill Crane Nesting Success and Recruitment in Northwest Colorado.* Grand Junction: Colorado Division of Wildlife, Terrestrial Wildlife Section.

Rhymer, J. M., M. G. Fain, J. E. Austin, D. H. Johnson, and C. Krajewski. 2001. Mitochondrial phylogeography, specific taxonomy, and conservation genetics of sandhill cranes (*Grus canadensis;* Aves: Gruidae). *Conservation Genetics* 2:201–18.

Safina, C. 1993. Population trends, habitat utilization, and outlook for the future of sandhill cranes in North America: A review and synthesis. *Bird Populations* 1:1–27.

Schlorff, R. W. 2005. Greater sandhill crane: Research and management in California since 1978. In *Proceedings of the Ninth National North American Workshop*, Sacramento, California, ed. F. Chavez-Ramirez, 155–65. Baraboo WI: North American Crane Working Group.

Schmitt, C. G., and B. Hale. 1997. Sandhill crane hunts in the Rio Grande Valley and southwest New Mexico. In *Proceedings of the Seventh North American Crane Workshop*, Biloxi, Mississippi, ed. R. P. Urbanek and D. W. Stahlecker, 219–31. Grand Island NE: North American Crane Working Group.

Semenchuk, G. R., ed. 1992. *Atlas of the Breeding Birds of Alberta.* Edmonton: Federation of Alberta Naturalists.

Sharp, D. E. 1995. *Status and Harvests of Sandhill Cranes: Mid-continent and Rocky Mountain Populations.* Internal report. Golden CO: U.S. Fish & Wildlife Service, Office of Migratory Bird Management.

Sharp. D. E., J. D. Dubovsky, and K. L. Kruse. 2003. *Status and Harvests of the Mid-continent and Rocky Mountain Populations of Sandhill Cranes.* Administrative report. Denver: U. S. Fish and Wildlife Service.

Sharp, D. E., and W. O. Vogel. 1992. Population status, hunting regulations, hunting activities, and harvest of mid-continental sandhill cranes. In *Proceedings of the Sixth North American Crane Workshop,* Regina, Alaska, ed. D. W. Stahlecker, 24–32. Grand Island NE: North American Crane Working Group.

Tacha, T. C., S. A. Nesbitt, and P. A. Vohs. 1992. *Sandhill Crane.* The Birds of North America, no. 31. Philadelphia: Academy of Natural Sciences, and Washington DC: American Ornithologists' Union.

———. 1994. Sandhill crane. In *Migratory Shore and Upland Game Bird Management in North Americas,* ed. T. C. Tacha. and C. E. Braun, 76–94. Washington DC: International Association of Fish and Wildlife Agencies.

Tacha, T. C., P. A. Vohs, and W. D. Ward. 1985. Morphometric variation of sandhill cranes from mid-continent North America. *Journal of Wildlife Management* 49:246–50.

Tebble, P. D., and C. D. Ankney. 1979. Biology of the sandhill cranes in the southern Algoma District of Ontario. In *Proceedings of the 1978 Crane Workshop,* Rockport, Texas, ed. J. C. Lewis, 129–34. Fort Collins: Colorado State University Printing Service.

Urbanek, R. P., J. W. Duff, S. R. Swengel, and L. A. Fondow. 2005. Reintroduction techniques: Post-release performance of sandhill cranes (1) released into wild flocks and (2) led on migration by ultralight aircraft. In *Proceedings of the Ninth North American Crane Workshop,* Sacramento, California, ed. F. Chavez-Ramirez, 203–11. Baraboo WI: North American Crane Working Group.

Walkinshaw, L. H. 1949. *The Sandhill Cranes.* Bulletin No. 29. Bloomfield Hills MI: Cranbrook Institute of Science.

———. 1965, A new sandhill crane from central Canada. *Canadian Field-Naturalist* 79:181–84.

Windingstad, R. M. 1988. Nonhunting mortality in the sandhill crane. *Journal of Wildlife Management* 52:260–63.

Zickafoose, J. 2008. Love and death among the cranes. *Bird Watcher's Digest* 21 (2): 9299.

Whooping Crane

Ackerman. J. 2004. "No mere bird." *National Geographic* 205 (4): 39–55.

Armbruster, M. J. 1990. Characterization of habitat used by whooping cranes during migration. *U.S. Dept. of Interior, Fish & Wildlife Service Biological Reports* 90 (4):1–16.

Austin, J. E., and A. L. Richert. 2001. *A Comprehensive Review of Observational and Site Evaluation Data of Migrant Whooping Cranes in the United States, 1943–99.* Jamestown ND: Northern Prairie Research Center.

———. 2005. Patterns of habitat use by whooping cranes during migration: Summary from 1977–1999 site data evaluation. In *Proceedings of the Ninth North American Crane Workshop,* Sacramento, California, ed. F. Chavez-Ramirez, 79–104. Baraboo WI: North American Crane Working Group.

Chavez-Ramirez, F. 2004. Whooping cranes in Nebraska: Historical and recent trends. *Braided River* 20:1–9.

Chavez-Ramirez, F., and R. D. Slack. 1999. Movements and flock characteristics of whooping cranes wintering on the Texas coast. *Texas Journal of Science* 51 (1): 3–14.

Conover, A. 1998. Fly away home. *Smithsonian* 29 (1): 62–70.

Ellis, D. H., G. F. Gee, K. R. Clegg, J. W. Duff, W. A. Lishman, and W. J. L. Sladen. 2001. Lessons from the motorized migrations. In *Proceedings of the Eighth North American Crane Workshop,* Albuquerque, New Mexico, ed. D. H. Ellis, 139–44. Seattle, WA: North American Crane Working Group.

Ellis, D. H., J. C. Lewis, G. F. Gee, and D. G. Smith. 2001.

Population recovery efforts of the whooping crane with emphasis on reintroduction efforts: Past and future. In *Proceedings of the Eighth North American Crane Workshop*, ed. D. H. Ellis, 142–50. Albuquerque, New Mexico. Seattle: North American Crane Working Group.

Folk, M. J., S. A. Nesbitt, S. T. Schwikert, J. A. Schmidt, K. A. Sullivan, T. J. Miller, S. B. Baynes, and J. M. Parker. 2005. Breeding biology of re-introduced non-migratory whooping cranes in Florida. In *Proceedings of the Ninth North American Crane Workshop*, Sacramento, California, ed. F. Chavez-Ramirez, 105–9. Baraboo WI: North American Crane Working Group.

Folk, M. J., S. A. Nesbitt, J. M. Parker, M. G. Spalding, S. B. Baynes, and K. L. Candelora. 2008. Current status of nonmigratory whooping cranes in Florida. In *Proceedings of the Tenth North American Crane Workshop*, Zacatecas City, Mexico, ed. M. J. Folk and S. A. Nesbitt, 7–12. Gambier OH: North American Crane Working Group.

Fondow, L. E. A. 2008. Winter habitat selection by a reintroduced population of migratory whooping cranes: Emerging patterns and implications for the future. In *Proceedings of the Tenth North American Crane Workshop*, Zacatecas City, Mexico, ed. M. J. Folk and S. A. Nesbitt, 152. Gambier OH: North American Crane Working Group.

Gil, K. 2007. The banded whooping cranes. *Braided River* 22:1–6.

Gil, K. 2009. One whooping crane's family tree. *Braided River*, 23:14–16.

Gil, K., W. E. Grant, R. D. Slack, and E. Weir. Age-specific survival, fecundity, and finite rate of increase in the endangered whooping crane (*Grus americana*). In review, *Condor*.

Horwich, R. H. 2001. Developing a migratory whooping crane flock. In *Proceedings of the Eighth North American Crane Workshop*, Albuquerque, New Mexico, ed. D. H.

134

Ellis, 85–95. Seattle: North American Crane Working Group.

Howe, M. A. 1987. Habitat use by migrating whooping cranes in the Aransas–Wood Buffalo corridor. In *Proceedings of the 1985 Crane Workshop*, Grand Island, Nebraska, ed. J. C. Lewis, 303–11. Grand Island NE: Platte River Whooping Crane Maintenance Trust and U. S. Fish & Wildlife Service.

Johns, B. W. 2005. Whooping cranes: The Canadian connection. *Braided River* 21:1–5.

Johns, B. W., J. P. Gossen, E. Kuyt, and L. Craig-Moore. 2005. Philopatry and dispersal in whooping cranes. In *Proceedings of the Ninth North American Crane Workshop*, Sacramento, California, ed. F. Chavez-Ramirez, 117–25. Baraboo WI: North American Crane Working Group.

Johnsgard, P. A., and R. Redfield. 1977. Sixty-five years of whooping crane records in Nebraska. *Nebraska Bird Review* 45:54–56.

Johnson, K. A. 1982. Whooping crane use of the Platte River, Nebraska: History, status and management recommendations. In *Proceedings of the 1981 Crane Workshop*, Tavernier, Florida, ed. J. C. Lewis, 33–44. Stillwater: Oklahoma State University.

Kuyt, E. 1992. Aerial radio-tracking of whooping cranes migrating between Wood Buffalo National Park and Aransas National Wildlife Refuge. *Canadian Wildlife Service Occasional Papers* 74:1–53.

———. 1993. Whooping crane, *Grus americana*, home range and breeding range expansion in Wood Buffalo National Park, 1970–1991. *Canadian Field-Naturalist* 107: 1–12.

Kuyt, E., and P. Goossen. 1987. Survival, age composition, sex ratio, and age of first breeding of whooping cranes. In *Proceedings of the 1985 Crane Workshop*, Grand Island, Nebraska, ed. J. C. Lewis, 230–44. Grand Island NE: Platte River Whooping Crane Maintenance Trust.

Lewis, J. C. 1993. *Whooping Crane.* The Birds of North America, no. 153. Philadelphia: Academy of Natural Sciences, and Washington DC: American Ornithologists' Union.

Lingle, G. R., K. J. Strom, and J. W. Ziewitz. 1986. Whooping crane roost site characteristics on the Platte River, Buffalo County, Nebraska. *Nebraska Bird Review* 54:36–39.

Lingle, G. R., G. A. Wingfield, and J. W. Ziewitz. 1991. The migration ecology of whooping cranes in Nebraska. In *Proceedings of the International Crane Foundation Workshop, 1987,* Qiqhar, People's Republic of China, ed. J. Harris, 395–401. Baraboo WI: International Crane Foundation.

Maguire, K. J. 2008. Habitat selection of reintroduced whooping cranes, *Grus americana,* on the breeding range. Master's thesis, University of Wisconsin, Madison.

Nesbitt, S., M. J. Folk, K. A. Sullivan, S. T. Schwikert, and M. G. Spalding. 2001. An update of the Florida whooping crane release project through June 2000. In *Proceedings of the Eighth North American Crane Workshop,* Albuquerque, New Mexico, ed. D. H. Ellis, 62–72. Seattle: North American Crane Working Group.

Pittman, C. 2003. Making whoopee. *Smithsonian* 33 (10): 92–95.

Richert, A. L. 1999. Multiple scale analyses of whooping crane habitat in Nebraska. PhD dissertation, University of Nebraska–Lincoln.

Schorff R. W. 2005. Greater sandhill crane research and management in California since 1978. In *Proceedings of the Ninth North American Crane Workshop,* Sacramento, California, ed. F. Chavez-Ramirez, 155–66. Baraboo WI: North American Crane Working Group.

Spalding, M. G., M. J. Folk, and S. A. Nesbitt. 2008. Reproductive health of the Florida flock of introduced whooping cranes. In *Proceedings of the Tenth North American Crane Workshop,* Zacatecas City, Mexico, ed. M. J. Folk and

S. A. Nesbitt, 154. Gambier OH: North American Crane Working Group.

Stap, D. 1998. A population reinstated: Establishing a new population of whooping cranes in central Florida improves the prospects for the birds' long-term survival. *Audubon* 100 (4): 92–97.

Stahlecker, D. W. 1997. Availability of stopover habitat to migrating whooping cranes in Nebraska. In *Proceedings of the Seventh North American Crane Workshop*, ed. R. P. Urbanek and D. W. Stahlecker, 132–40. Grand Island NE: North American Crane Working Group.

Stehn, T. V. 1992. Unusual movements and behavior of color-banded whooping cranes during winter. In *Proceedings of the Sixth North American Crane Workshop*, Regina, Saskatchewan, ed. D. W. Stahlecker and R. P. Urbanek, 95–101. Grand Island NE: North American Crane Working Group.

Stehn, T. V., and T. Wassenich. 2008. Whooping crane collisions with power lines: An issue paper. In *Proceedings of the Tenth North American Crane Workshop*, Zacatecas City, Mexico, ed. M. J. Folk and S. A. Nesbitt, 25–36. Gambier OH: North American Crane Working Group.

Thoemke, K. W., and P. M. Prior. 2004. A crane called Lucky: A major milestone in the reintroduction of whooping cranes to Florida. *Living Bird* 23 (1): 28–35.

Urbanek, R. P., and L. E. A. Fondow. 2008. Survival, movements, social structure and reproductive behavior during development of a population of reintroduced whooping cranes. In *Proceedings of the Tenth North American Crane Workshop*, Zacatecas City, Mexico, ed. M. J. Folk and S. A. Nesbitt, 155. Gambier OH: North American Crane Working Group.

Westwood, C. M., and F. Chavez-Ramirez. 2005. Patterns of food use of wintering whooping cranes on the Texas coast. In *Proceedings of the Ninth North American Crane Workshop*,

Sacramento, California, ed. Chavez-Ramirez, 133–40. Baraboo WI: North American Crane Working Group.

The Platte River Valley and Rainwater Basin

Brown, C. R., and M. B. Brown, 2001. *Birds of the Cedar Point Biological Station.* Cedar Point Biological Station Occasional Papers. Lincoln NE: Cedar Point Biological Station. http://digitalcommons.unl.edu/biosciornithology/24 (accessed April 21, 2010).

Colt, C. J. 1996. Breeding bird use of riparian forests along the central Platte River: A spacial analysis. Master's thesis, University of Nebraska–Lincoln.

Committee on Endangered and Threatened Species in the Platte River Basin. 2005. *Endangered and Threatened Species in the Platte River.* Washington DC: National Academies Press.

Cunningham, D. 1983. River portraits: The Platte. NEBRASKA-*land* 63 (1): 29–30.

Currier, P. J., G. R. Lingle, and J. G. VanDerwalker. 1985. *Migratory Bird Habitat on the Platte and North Platte Rivers in Nebraska.* Grand Island NE: Platte River Whooping Crane Habitat Maintenance Trust.

Dahl, T. E. 1990. *Wetlands: Losses in the United States 1780's to 1980's.* Washington DC: U.S. Dept. of Interior, Fish & Wildlife Service.

Davis, C. A. 2005a. Breeding bird communities in riparian forests along the central Platte River, Nebraska. *Great Plains Research* 15:199–211.

——. 2005b. Breeding and migration bird use of a riparian woodland along the Platte River in central Nebraska. *North American Bird Bander,* July–September, 2005, 109–14.

Faanes, C. E., and G. R. Lingle. 1995. Breeding birds of the Platte Valley of Nebraska. Northern Prairie Wildlife Research Center, Jamestown ND, http://www.npwrc.usgs

.gov/resources/distr/birds/platte/platte (page discontinued).

Gordon, C. C., L. D. Flake, and K. F. Higgins. 1990. Aquatic invertebrates in the Rainwater Basin, Nebraska. *Prairie Naturalist* 22:191–200.

Jenkins, A., ed. 1993. *The Platte River: An Atlas of the Big Bend Region.* Kearney: University of Nebraska–Kearney.

Johnsgard, P. A. 2001. *The Nature of Nebraska: Ecology and Biodiversity.* Lincoln: University of Nebraska Press.

———. 2007. The Platte: River of dust or river of dreams? *Prairie Fire* 1 (5): 12–13, 17–19.

———. 2008. *The Platte: Channels in Time.* 2nd ed. Lincoln: University of Nebraska Press.

———. 2009. "The birds of Nebraska." University of Nebraska–Lincoln, Digital Commons, http://digitalcommons.unl.edu/biosciornithology/38 (accessed April 21, 2010).

Johnson, W. C. 1961. Woodland expansion in the Platte River, Nebraska: Patterns and causes. *Ecological Monographs* 64:45–84.

Jorgensen, J. G. 2004. An overview of the shorebird migration in the eastern Rainwater Basin, Nebraska. *Nebraska Ornithologists' Union Occasional Papers* no. 8:1–68.

Krapu, G., ed. 1981. *The Platte River Ecology Study: Special Research Report.* Jamestown ND: Northern Prairie Wildlife Research Station, U.S. Fish & Wildlife Service.

LaGrange, T. 2005. *Guide to Nebraska's Wetlands and their Conservation Needs,* 2nd ed. Lincoln: Nebraska Game and Parks Commission.

Line, L. 2007. New dawn for a prairie river. *National Wildlife,* October–November 2007, 22–29.

Lingle, G. R. 1994. *Birding Crane River: Nebraska's Platte.* Grand Island NE: Harrier.

Mollhoff, W. J. 2000. *The Nebraska Breeding Bird Atlas.* Lincoln: Nebraska Game and Parks Commission.

Nagel, H. G., K. Geisler, J. Cochran, J. Fallesen, B. Hadenfelt,

J. Mathews, J. Nickel, S. Stec, and A. Walters. 1980. Platte River island succession. *Transactions Nebraska Academy of Sciences* 8:77–90.

Scharf, W., J. Kren, L. R. Brown, and P. A Johnsgard. 2008. Body weights and distributions of birds in Nebraska's central and western Platte Valley. University of Nebraska–Lincoln, Digital Commons, http://digitalcommons.unl .edu/biosciornithology/43.

Sharpe, R., W. R. Silcock, and J. G. Jorgensen. 2001. *The Birds of Nebraska, Their Distribution and Temporal Occurrence*, Lincoln: University of Nebraska Press.

Smith, C. 2007. The Platte River Recovery Implementation Program: Adaptive management and collaboration on the Platte. *Prairie Fire* 1 (6): 12–14.

Van der Valk, A., ed. 1989. *Northern Prairie Wetlands.* Ames: Iowa State University Press.

Suggested Reading

Doughty, R. W. 1989. *Return of the Whooping Crane.* Austin: University of Texas Press. An account of efforts to save the Aransas–Wood Buffalo flock of whooping cranes through the late 1980s.

Forsberg, M. 2004. *On Ancient Wings: The Sandhill Cranes of North America.* Lincoln NE: Michael Forsberg Photography. A beautifully illustrated firsthand account and photographic essay of the sandhill crane, involving travels from Alaska to Cuba.

Grooms, G. 1991. *Cry of the Sandhill Crane.* Minocqua WI: North Word Press. A non-technical, photographically illustrated account of sandhill cranes.

Hughes, J. 2008. *Cranes: A Natural History of a Bird in Crisis.* Tonawanda NY: Firefly Books. The most comprehensive history of the struggle to save the whooping crane. There is also an authoritative and beautifully illustrated general account of cranes and their biology, including short descriptions of all the other cranes of the world, with range maps and population estimates as of about 2005.

Hyde, D. 1968. *Sandy: The True Story of a Sandhill Crane that Joined Our Family.* New York: Doubleday. An account of raising a greater sandhill crane on an Oregon ranch, by a master storyteller.

Jensen, P. J. 2000. *Legends of the Crane.* Denver: Sandstones Press. Poems and legends about cranes from around the world.

Johnsgard, P. A. 1981. *Those of the Gray Wind: The Sandhill Cranes.* New York: Doubleday. Four short stories of the interactions of four children of varied cultures with sandhill cranes, set at four different times in American history between 1860 and 1980.

———. 1983. *Cranes of the World*. Bloomington: Indiana University Press. A technical monograph of the cranes of the world and their biology.

———. 1991. *Crane Music: A Natural History of American Cranes*. Washington DC: Smithsonian Institution Press. A natural history of the sandhill and whooping cranes, and a brief overview of the world's other cranes.

———. 2008. *The Platte: Channels in Time*. 2nd ed. Lincoln: University of Nebraska Press. The Platte's natural and human history, and associated conservation issues.

Katz, B. 1993. *So Cranes May Dance*. Chicago: Chicago Review Press. The history of the International Crane Foundation.

Lewis, J. C. 1993. *Whooping crane*. The Birds of North America, no. 153. Philadelphia: Academy of Natural Sciences, and Washington DC: American Ornithologists' Union. A technical summary of the biology of the whooping crane.

Mathiessen, P. 2001. *The Birds of Heaven: Travels with Cranes*. New York: North Point Press. An account of seeing the cranes of the world, authored by a well-known nature writer and illustrated by Robert Bateman.

McCoy, J. J. 1966. *The Hunt for the Whooping Cranes: A Natural History Detective Story*. New York: Lothrop, Lee and Shepard. Recounts the long search for the cranes' nesting grounds.

McNulty, F. 1996. *The Whooping Crane: The Bird that Defies Extinction*. New York: E. P. Dutton. A history of the efforts to save the whooping crane though the early 1990s.

Pratt, J. 1996. *The Whooping Crane: North America's Symbol of Conservation*. Prescott AZ: Castle Rock. An account of conservation efforts for the whooping crane.

Price, A. L. 2001. *Cranes; The Noblest Flyers, in Natural History and Cultural Lore*. Albuquerque: La Alameda Press. A collection of crane myths, folklore and cultural history.

Sakrison, D. 2007. *Chasing the Ghost Birds: Saving Swans and Cranes from Extinction.* Ripon WI: Watson Street Press. A recent account of efforts to save several endangered species, including the whooping crane.

Schoff, G. 2007. *Reflections: The Story of Cranes.* 2nd ed. Baraboo WI: International Crane Foundation. A brief illustrated review of the cranes of the world and the work of the International Crane Foundation.

Tacha, T. C., S. A. Nesbitt, and P. A. Vohs. 1992. *Sandhill crane.* The Birds of North America, no. 31. Philadelphia: Academy of Natural Sciences, and Washington DC: American Ornithologists' Union. A technical summary of the biology of the sandhill crane.

Von Treuenfels, C.-A. 2006. *The Magic of Cranes.* New York: Harry Abrams. An authoritative account of crane biology by an internationally known German conservationist, with the author's spectacular photographs of wild cranes from around the world.

Walkinshaw, L. H. 1949. The sandhill cranes. *Cranbrook Institute of Sciences Bulletin* 29:1-202. A relatively early technical summary of the biology of the sandhill crane.

———. 1973. *Cranes of the World.* New York: Winchester Press. An early monograph of the cranes of the world.

143

Online Sources of Information on Cranes

Refuges and Sanctuaries

Aransas National Wildlife Refuge (Austwell, Texas): http://www.fws.gov/southwest/REFUGES/texas/aransas

Bernard W. Baker Sanctuary (Bellevue, Michigan): http://www.bakersanctuary.org

Bosque Del Apache National Wildlife Refuge (Socorro, New Mexico): http://www.fws.gov/southwest/refuges/newmex/bosque

Lillian Annette Rowe Sanctuary (Gibbon, Nebraska): http://www.rowesanctuary.org

Mississippi Sandhill Crane National Wildlife Refuge (Gautier, Mississippi): http://www.fws.gov/mississippisandhillcrane

Necedah National Wildlife Refuge (Necedah, Wisconsin): http://midwest.fws.gov/necedah

Wood Buffalo National Park (Alberta and Northwest Territories, Canada): http://www.pc.gc.ca/pn-np/nt/woodbuffalo/index

Conservation Groups and Agencies

Canadian Wildlife Service: http://www.cws-scf.ec.gc.ca

Center for Conservation Research (Calgary Zoo): http://www.calgaryzoo.org

Environment Canada (general whooping crane information): http://www.pnr-rpn.ec.gc.ca/nature/endspecies/whooping/index.en.html

International Crane Foundation (Baraboo, Wisconsin): http://www.savingcranes.org

The Majestic and Endangered Whooping Crane (general

information and many links): http://raysweb.net/special places/pages/crane.html

National Audubon Society: http://www.audubon.org

National Geographic Crane Cam (live streaming video from Rowe Sanctuary on the Platte during spring): http://ngm.nationalgeographic.com/static-legacy/ngm/cranecam

National Wildlife Federation: http://www.nwf.org

Nebraska Birding Trails: http://www.nebraskabirdingtrails.com

North American Crane Working Group (publishes the *Unison Call*, a semiannual newsletter summarizing changes in crane populations: P.O. Box 566, Gambier OH 43022); http://www.nacwg.org

Northern Prairie Wildlife Research Center (U.S. Fish and Wildlife Service): http://www.npwrc.usgs.gov

Operation Crane Watch (migrations via satellite telemetry): http://www.npwrc.usgs.gov/resources/birds/cranemov

Operation Migration: http://www.operationmigration.org

Patuxent Wildlife Research Center (Laurel, Maryland): http://www.pwrc.usgs.gov/birds

Platte River Whooping Crane Maintenance Trust (Wood River, Nebraska): http://www.whoopingcrane.org

U.S. Fish and Wildlife Service: http://www.fws.gov

West Coast Crane Working Group: http://www.wccwg.nacwg.org

Whooping Crane Conservation Association (publishes *Grus Americana*, a periodic newsletter summarizing whooping crane population news): http://www.whoopingcrane.com

Whooping Crane Eastern Partnership (WCEP): http://www.bringbackthecranes.org

Literature References

Comprehensive Crane Bibliography (one of several digital library resources available through the International Crane Foundation library): http://www.savingcranes .org/comprehensivecranebibliography.html

Cranes of the World (Paul A. Johnsgard, Indiana University Press, 1979): http://digitalcommons.unl.edu/biosci cranes/1

Sandhill Crane (*Grus canadensis*):

http://digitalcommons.unl.edu/bioscicranes/25

Whooping Crane (*Grus americana*):

http://digitalcommons.unl.edu/bioscicranes/31

Classification and Evolution:

http://digitalcommons.unl.edu/bioscicranes/7

Individualistic and Social Behavior:

http://digitalcommons.unl.edu/bioscicranes/20

Vocalizations:

http://digitalcommons.unl.edu/bioscicranes/28

Ecology and Population Dynamics:

http://digitalcommons.unl.edu/bioscicranes/14

Comparative Reproductive Biology:

http://digitalcommons.unl.edu/bioscicranes/9

Endangered Species and Conservation:

http://digitalcommons.unl.edu/bioscicranes/15

Cranes in Myth and Legend:

http://digitalcommons.unl.edu/bioscicranes/11

References:

http://digitalcommons.unl.edu/bioscicranes/24

The Cranes: Status Survey and Action Plan (C. D. Meine and G. W. Archibald, editors, International Union for Conservation of Nature and Natural Resources, 1996): http:// www.npwrc.usgs.gov/resource/birds/cranes/index .htm

147

Index

This index does not include references to material found in the appendix. Illustrations (figures and maps) are indicted by bold.

154